MAMA SANG HYMNS

The Story of My Journey of Faith

This is my story ♫
This is my song ♪
Bonnie

BONNIE CORLISS HAIN

Exulon ELITE

MAMA SANG HYMNS
The Story of My Journey of Faith
by Bonnie Corliss Hain

Cover Design by Chris Hain

Printed in the United States of America.

ISBN 9781498427180

Unless otherwise indicated, Scripture quotations taken from the King James Version (KJV) – public domain.

www.xulonpress.com

DEDICATED TO:

Robin who made me promise to write my story.

and

Ann who asked me to type her story and thereby

gave me courage to write my own story.

ENDORSEMENTS

. . . *As I've said for so long, you have a story to tell and you're so capable of telling it in an interesting and honest way. Now I don't have to say that any more! Thank you for writing it!! I must tell you- I wanted to keep reading and reading. Even tho I already knew the story. You definitely held my interest. And, Dick's comments help to make it"real"!! They add a lot. Great idea to include them.* **Marylyn Link (Dick's sister)**

Your book arrived a few days ago and I had intended to just scan it, then put it aside to read it later, but you sucked me right in! I read the whole thing cover to cover on Saturday afternoon and have read it again today.

..You have a really good sense of pacing, sentence structure, sentence variation in terms of length and complexity, and are a natural storyteller. You know how to build up to a dramatic moment, how to include sensory details so the reader really feels like they are there with you in the story. You're good at describing other people but don't belabor their qualities or go on and on. You move well through the decades and even though your story covers many years, I never felt confused about where I was in time....I enjoyed it very much and learned some things about you that I didn't know.

I especially enjoyed visualizing you as a young girl and a teenager, along with the store, the dance classes, and all that responsibility you had as the Sunday school superintendent.

What people who don't write about their lives miss out on is the satisfaction of not only re-living their lives and writing about them, but the kindness one can bestow on their younger self. **Mardi Jo Link, niece, author of "When Evil Came to Good Hart," "Isadore's Secret," "Bootstrapper" and "Wicked Takes The Witness Stand".**

I'm wiping tears after reading your book and seeing God's grace in your life story...Your words have life and aliveness, as you write in your heart language. Truly, as I've said so many times, God has gifted you in words and in expression...your and Dick's writing together enhances the drama of your lives individually and together...I'm so thrilled you have this narrative of your life and God's presence in writing now...may He get the glory! I know this is your desire and the desire of all your Jesus loving family and friends. **Thank you for sharing it with me! Delores Vincent**

Your book is straightforward, open and honest. It is very real and you do not shy away from the truth. Your poetry is rich. It will touch many lives. I love that Dick offered his part/version at various times and this too is different and adds another layer of realness to your mutual walk of faith and life. The cover artwork is fantastic! All in all, nice work, Bonnie!!! Let me know when it's available and I expect a signed copy!! **Ron Gelaude, interim pastor at our new church, author of "The Religion of Jesus" and "Crazy Shepherd, Crazy Sheep."**

TABLE OF CONTENTS

INTRODUCTION

In 1963 when I was twenty-nine years old, I had an OFFICIAL nervous breakdown. The criterion for an OFFICIAL nervous breakdown is that you have to have been hospitalized for it. If you do it all at home, it doesn't count. Because I was suicidal, I spent six weeks in the locked ward of the psychiatric wing in the same hospital where my second son had been born. I had electric shock treatments that knocked me out, calmed me down, destroyed portions of my memory, and caused me to have "charley horses" (leg cramps) for the next several years. In 1965 a police ambulance took me to Milwaukee County General Hospital where I heard Billy Graham for the first time.

This is my story about my journey of faith. It is the story God gave me to tell. It is His-story. My history is His story....how He wooed me and won me and never gave up on me even when I gave up on Him and tried to get away from Him. Like the psalmist, my heart overflows with a Godly theme.

Chapter 1

MEARS YEARS

$\mathscr{I}$ was born in 1934. I was born again in 1965. Mama sang hymns while she was pregnant for me.

PRETTY MAMA

Mama was a very pretty woman. Once a week during the winter when Daddy closed our store at noon, Mama would put on make-up (that Daddy called her "war paint") and we went out to eat and see a movie. I always watched with curious fascination as she powdered her face, rouged her cheeks, and put on lipstick. I watched with wonderment and pride as my mama became as beautiful as any movie star. Daddy and I were proud of Mama's prettiness.

Mama Age 16

I often wondered if I would be pretty when I grew up. I desperately hoped so, but when I looked at myself in a mirror, I knew I was not pretty.

Daddy's sister Ruth loved to tease me about Daddy's first glimpse of Mama and me together in the bed where she had pushed all 10 pounds of me out into the world without benefit of medicine or hospital. According to Aunt Ruth, Daddy had looked at his wife and newborn daughter lying together in the bed where I'd been born, and exclaimed, "Isn't she BEAUTIFUL!" Then Aunt Ruth's punch line: he was NOT referring to me.

Mama & Me

MEARS FOOD CENTER

I was a grocer's daughter. Daddy had a 7-day-a-week general merchandise store. An impressive neon sign "MEARS FOOD CENTER"

Dad & Mom

hung above the front door: We lived in a cement block addition in back of our store. I used to wonder how people got along without having a store attached to their house when they needed something.

When Mama didn't know what to fix for lunch or supper, each of us could pick out a can of soup or stew or potted meat or whatever hit our fancy and fix our own individual meal.

On Sunday evenings after returning home from the movies, we would sneak through the door

Dad & Mom & Me

between our house and the back of the store (careful not to be seen by any potential customers who might want Daddy to open the store for a few minutes for their convenience) and choose what we would have for our evening snack. I would usually have two scoops of ice-cream topped with chocolate sauce, marshmallow sauce (made from melted marshmallows carefully melted in a pan above boiling water in a double boiler) and topped off with a bright red maraschino cherry. I would then enjoy my custom sundae in my bedroom beside my tiny white Arvin radio, listening to my favorite Sunday night programs (such as "Baby Snooks," "Henry Aldrich," "Edgar Bergen and Charley McCarthy," "Corliss Archer," "The Shadow," etc.)

Before the Great Depression Daddy had managed a Kroger store and a Piggly Wiggly store. During the Great Depression he had done farm work in exchange for food, housing, and not much pay. After he'd met and married Mama, he'd clerked in his brother's store in Hart, Michigan. In 1939 he sold our little house in Hart and bought our store in Mears, about 3 miles west of Hart.

1939 became a big year for our family of four. Mama had me and my baby brother Dickie baptized in the Hart Methodist Episcopal Church.

She taught me to kneel by my bed and say an alarming little prayer: "Now I lay me down to sleep. I pray the Lord my soul to keep. If I should die before I wake, I pray the Lord my soul to take." The last part was very scary for me..

Soon after Baby Dickie and I were baptized, we moved to Mears.

Our Store

SUNDAY SCHOOL

I began attending primary Sunday School in the Mears Methodist Episcopal Church across the road from our store. For the first time in my life I heard that Jesus loved me and was coming to get me, so I should be watching and waiting for His arrival. I went home and sat in the yard and watched and waited for Him to show up. I wholeheartedly obeyed all the truth I knew about Him. He had me hooked for the rest of my life.

I continued in spiritual gestation prior to rebirth for another 26 years.

Mears Church

INVITING JESUS IN

During my childhood days in the Mears two-room school, Child Evangelism people periodically presented flannel graph Bible stories, and while every head was bowed and every eye was closed, I unfailingly raised my hand to signal my willingness to invite Jesus into my heart

When I was in eighth grade and had finally quit wetting the bed, I went to Methodist youth camp on Hamlin Lake near Ludington.. The last night at camp I went forward during a campfire altar call. I prayed the sinner's prayer and invited Jesus into my heart again.

I went forward for three reasons: I was genuinely hungry to know Jesus more, I didn't want to be the only kid in camp who didn't go forward that night, and I had a crush on the preacher who had issued the altar call.

People at Mears Methodist Church heard the good news and rejoiced and urged me to officially become a member of the church. My parents warned me that they wanted only my money. They tried to talk me out of joining. I joined anyway.

SECRETARY, SUPERINTENDENT

I became Sunday School Secretary and kept track of attendance and offerings until, for lack of candidates I was asked to become Sunday School Superintendent when I was sixteen. I served in that capacity till I went away to college 2 years later.

Every week I walked across the road and sorted out the lesson sheets for the next Sunday service. I selected the hymns, and I stood up in front and led the singing. I loved the hymns, and I loved the limelight. I felt cherished and special. Sometimes I played the piano while everyone filed out to their age-appropriate Sunday School classes. Church (not Sunday School) was still boring for me, and the Bible still didn't make sense to me.

OUR FAMILY AND CHURCH

My parents didn't go to church. Mama's family didn't go to church. Daddy's family went to church a lot. He and several of his siblings had rebelled against their childhood experiences in church.

Daddy was the next to last child born into a family of 7 sons and 2 daughters. His mother had been nineteen when she married a 45-year-old man. They'd produced 9 children before the grandfather I never knew died and left the family in poverty. Daddy's mother also died before Daddy met Mama.

When his mother died, Daddy dropped out of high school during his senior year and rode the rails, bumming across the country with one of his brothers.

Uncle Leo, Daddy's youngest brother, went to live with a Christian doctor who mentored him and later delivered me. Uncle Leo became a Wesleyan Methodist preacher. I'm quite sure that Dr. Griffin probably prayed for me. I know Uncle Leo and Aunt Vera prayed for me.

When I was eight, Aunt Vera gave me piano lessons in the Wesleyan parsonage. I paid her twenty-five cents each lesson. One day when Mama was late to pick me up, and I was waiting just inside the parsonage door for her, I witnessed a wondrous sight in the adjoining room: Uncle Leo and Aunt Vera were on their knees praying out loud together ! I had never seen such a thing. It stuck in my memory for the rest of my life.

In those days there was a radio program that repeated the theme: "The family that prays together stays together." This was the first time I'd ever seen it happen in real life.

MAMA'S HYMNS

Mama sang hymns at home. "The Old Rugged Cross," "The Church in the Wildwood," "Happy Day When Jesus Washed My Sins Away," "Love Lifted Me," "Softly and Tenderly Jesus Is Calling," "In the Garden," "What a Friend We Have In Jesus," etc. She sang while she did dishes. She sang while she cleaned house. I'm sure I heard her singing hymns for nine months before I was born.

Now I sing while I do dishes, and I sing while I work around the house. Hymns inhabit the deepest part of my mind. They regularly and involuntarily pop up to accompany and comment upon whatever is going on in my life at any given moment. They are my native language singing silently inside my head.

Mama had learned her hymns during the first fourteen years of her life when she had attended Sunday School and church revival meetings in Indiana.

MAMA'S MEN

In 1928 when she was fourteen she and her family left Indiana and moved to Michigan where she fell in love and got married as soon as she'd finished ninth grade. She hardly ever went to church again after that.

During the Great Depression Mama and her first husband went without food in their house for three days. So he left her and returned to Illinois to live with his family. He told Mama to go back to her family. Many years later I asked Mama why he hadn't taken her with him, and she told me that in those days you couldn't take another mouth home to be fed.

The divorce broke Mama's heart and scarred her for the rest of her life.

When she was nineteen, she met and married Daddy. I was born just before her twenty-first birthday.

MAMA and ME

I was the first grandchild, born when Grandma was thirty-six and had five young children still living at home. Uncle Charles was exactly one year older than I. He and I were playmates. Sometimes Aunt Ethelyn let me play with her wedding paper dolls. I loved visiting them in "The Block" in downtown Hart.

I was an "only child" for five years and an "only daughter" for almost twelve years. Mama doted on me. I basked in my privileged life as a much-wanted child.

Before she met Daddy, Mama had worked in a shirt factory in Hart and was an excellent seamstress. She sewed beautiful clothes for me. She made me little dresses with matching bloomers. She made me costumes to wear in Golden Fair parades in Mears. She made me costumes to wear in dance recitals. She made drapes with matching bedspreads and dressing table skirts that transformed my bedrooms into places fit for princesses. When I was in college, she made me a beautiful formal dress like one I had admired in a movie.

GROWING UP IN MEARS

Mears was a wonderful place to live. I adored Ruth A., my teacher in the primary room of the two-room school. I believed she was the most beautiful woman I'd ever seen, except for my beautiful mother who was by far the prettiest mother anywhere. Miss A's beauty flowed from her affectionate smile. I loved school.

Mears School

My life revolved around school, Sunday School, and our store. I've always loved the limelight. My voice carried. I got lots of "pieces" to say in the annual school and Sunday School programs. Both parents were always there to see me perform.

One thing bothered me when Mama came to church to see me and my siblings perform in programs: Mama never sang hymns in church! When I nudged her and pointed to the hymnal, she just shook her head and said she couldn't sing. Well, how come she could sing hymns at home but not in church? I'm still scratching my head about that question.

I won every award given for perfect Sunday School attendance. During each Christmas program I proudly marched to the front of the sanctuary to receive recognition.

When I was nine, I graduated from Hilma Johnson's primary class into Flora Riley's "junior girls" Sunday School class. Every summer Flora hosted her Sunday School girls for a day at "Rileys' Roost," their summer cottage on Silver Lake. She served us delicious hot chocolate with vanilla in it. Every time I have hot chocolate, I put vanilla in it and think of dear Flora Riley. I remember her telling us in all seriousness that we must never put anything on top of our Bibles. To this day I usually don't put anything on top of my many Bibles.

When I was twelve, I advanced to Alice Augur's "intermediate girls" Sunday School class. Alice seemed to love us even more than Hilma and Flora. Alice had been crippled from polio when she was five, and she walked with two crutches. She always had a big smile on her face and love in her eyes. When I roller-skated past the little office where her parents had "Mrs. Augur's Kanning Kitchen," I counted on Alice's loving smile and friendly wave to me as I happily skated by.

Hilma, Flora, and Alice gave rewards for Scripture memorization, and I learned Psalm 1, Psalm 23, Psalm 100, 1 Corinthians 13 (the whole chapter), Philippians 4:8, and also the entire list of the books of the Old Testament. But when I tried to read the Bible, it didn't make sense to me until 1965 when I was thirty-one. I'll tell about that later.

Hilma died while I was in high school. Alice died in an auto accident while I was in tenth grade. Alice had been my piano teacher for several years, as well as my Sunday School teacher. I loved her very much. Ruth A., my loving and beautiful primary school teacher attended my wedding in 1954. I have always felt strong devotion to her.

During the years when I was Sunday School Superintendent, my Sunday School teacher's daughter Grace played the organ. One weekend Grace and I attended a Methodist Youth Rally in Big Rapids. We stayed in a private home, and I remember being in the balcony of the Big Rapids Methodist Church that Sunday morning singing "May Jesus

Christ Be Praised" with a large group of Michigan Methodist young people. Every time I hear that hymn I nostalgically remember that long-ago Sunday.

Grace and I directed the annual week of Vacation Bible School .

METHODIST GUIDELINES

One year an official from the Methodist Church hierarchy visited our church and objected to my active involvement in leadership while I was a tap and ballet dance teacher.

At that time dancing, drinking alcohol, and movies were officially not good things for good Methodists.

For a few Sundays I had experimented with staying home from movie matinees while my family went without me, and that had not felt right at all.

Make-up was not a good thing for a good Methodist girl to use, but that created no problem for me. Until I went away to college, I felt uncomfortable wearing lipstick (much less anything more elaborate).

My journey of faith faced serious challenges at home where Daddy considered the Bible to be full of fairy tales and myths while church goers were mostly hypocrites. He often commented that if Jesus Christ Himself ever showed up in person, He wouldn't be welcome in most churches.

PUBERTY

When I was twelve, Mother Nature interrupted my happy child-hood with embarrassing breasts, pubic hair, and my first menstrual period. Suddenly, two trusted males in my life stared at my developing body and made confusing comments with sexual overtones that made me squirm with discomfort and dismay. Increasingly, inappropriate touching became a regular occurrence when I happened to be alone with either of them. I felt guilty and soiled. The violated boundaries of my inexperienced innocence opened psychological gates for future destructive behavior to pour through.

When I was in my late thirties my friend Ann invited me to accom-pany her to a week of Christian meetings with a group called "Camps

Farthest Out." One of the speakers specialized in something called "healing of memories." I happened to mention to Ann about my childhood sexual abuse, and Ann insisted that I make an appointment with the "healing of memories" person. In those days people did not talk openly about such things. Secrecy and shielded reputations were the order of the day. Besides, what would be the use of bringing shame upon respected citizens in our small town? They would never live it down. Mother often admonished, "Be careful what you say. I have to live here."

One wise lady who was 30 years older than I and a respected Christian mentor to many besides me, shared with me her own painful childhood experience of being sexually abused. She told her father. Her father took the abuser to court. And after resultant public exposure to the shameful encounter, local mothers refused to let their daughters play with my friend. So my friend grew up without playmates because local parents chose to protect their daughters from spending time with "damaged goods."

Through the years I have been ministered to by people who prayed "healing of the memories" prayers with me. I have chosen to forgive my abusers as I live with the scars remaining inside me. My unhappy experiences open doors of ministry for me to pray with and for people who have suffered similar abuse. 2 Corinthians 1:4 says that we may be able to comfort others with the comfort we have personally received. I think that one of the very helpful factors is knowing that the abuse was not our fault and that we are not the only ones to have been sexually abused.

At the onset of my monthly cycles my parents sat me down in the antique swivel desk chair in the back end of our store, and while I stared at my toes and made myself not run away, they told me "the facts of life." I refused to believe and tried to forget what they said. Not the best day of my life...

Mama passed on to me the best advice she knew to give me: "Men only want ONE THING. They can't help themselves. Once they reach a certain point, they can't stop. It's all up to the woman." My dearest friend who is my age told me that her father had counseled her: "Don't let a man into your pants till you're married."

In school a male classmate pushed before my horrified gaze a pornographic cartoon of Popeye and Olive Oyl doing unspeakable things, and I burned with embarrassment. Life was getting very complicated

21

for me. My self esteem took a nosedive. I dreaded the monthly menstrual flow that stained my clothing when I forgot to change my clumsy, bulky, sanitary pads. I bent over double with cramps that accompanied that time of the month.

There's a Christmas song about 'Toyland, Toyland, dear little girl and boy land. Once you pass its borders, you can ne'er return again." I was not a little girl anymore. I was a budding sex object.

I could run faster than any other girls and most of the boys in Mears Elementary School. After the gravel roads in Mears had been blacktopped, I clamped on my roller skates and skated all day long from one end of Mears to the other. I loved climbing trees and showing off my athletic prowess. My preadolescent boy-friend threw the equivalent of a pail of water on my girlish pride when he slyly informed me that he'd looked up my shorts while I was showing off for him. I wanted to fall through a hole in the ground. I wanted to run away. But there was no escape for a budding sex object

HIGH SCHOOL

After eighth grade we were bused to Hart for high school. I felt like an outsider looking in. From being "a big fish in a little pond," I became "a little fish in a big pond." From having eight in my class, I went into a class of eighty. My self-confidence plummeted.

My boyfriend was one of the top athletes in our high school, and I took my identity from his success. I was his girl-friend, and everyone knew it. He was extremely possessive and did not allow me to talk with any other boys, and he was jealous of my girl-friends. He punished me by getting mad at me and refusing to talk to me. I spent most of my senior skip trip in my cabin crying because he was mad at me.

When my boy friend got his drivers license and invited me to go on a ride with him, I had no idea what he was doing when he took me on a country road, parked, put a blanket on the ground and stole my virginity. It didn't hurt. It didn't feel good. It felt shameful and frightening. It wasn't one of those things I could run home and tell Mama, "Guess what happened to me today!"

In those days one of the worst things that could happen was to get pregnant and have to get married. The shame lasted a lifetime. No one ever forgot. Aunt Ruth had a line for it: "There's the caught and the uncaught." Fortunately, I was one of the uncaught. My boyfriend married twice and never did have children.

I buried myself in books and homework. With all A's and one B average I became co-salutatorian of Hart High School's graduating class of 1952.

Mama believed in young marriages. She bought us a diamond ring through the wholesale catalog in our store. Someday we would pay her for it. She bought a good used car so I would have reliable transportation after I'd graduated from high school. My boy-friend drove my car all summer. It would be our car after we got married at Christmas time.

I began to have doubts about wanting to marry my boy-friend, but I believed that since we'd had sex, we were obligated to get married.

Chapter 2

MAGICAL YEARS

1952 became one of the most significant and memorable years of my entire life. I became "Miss Oceana County" and placed in the top 3 in the "Miss Michigan" contest. I became R.O.T.C. Kaydette at Central Michigan College of Education. Best of all, I met the man I would marry and became Sweetheart of his fraternity at Purdue University.

Aunt Ruth played a key role in my meeting Dick Hain. Here's how it happened: After Aunt Ruth and Uncle Tom had retired from the phone company in Muskegon, they'd bought a cottage on Duck Lake where they invited nieces and nephews to visit them and enjoy the lake. In 1952 Dick's parents were building their dream house on the lot next to Aunt Ruth's cottage. They used Aunt Ruth's phone until they could get a phone of their own in this newly-developing area.

I was at Duck Lake sunbathing on Aunt Ruth's dock with another eighteen-year-old girl from a nearby

Miss Oceana County

Aunt Ruth

cottage when Dick Hain and his cousin came by in their canoe. My new friend and I were so busy getting acquainted that we never noticed the boys shouting and splashing in their canoe, pretending they were drowning.

That night Aunt Ruth said that if we didn't pay attention to those boys, they were going to drown themselves. The next day they came again. We smiled at them. They took that to be an invitation to paddle over to our dock. They invited us to go on a canoe ride. We went. Thus Dick Hain swept me off my feet while I was wearing my diamond ring. He made me feel beautiful, fascinating, desirable, extraordinarily special, and quite confused. I'd never felt that way before. We were mutually smitten and quickly fell in love.

However, Dick Hain was a Boy Scout with a strong sense of honor, and he would not touch me while the diamond ring was still on my finger. Obviously, the ring had to go. When I gave it back to my boy friend the first time, he cried. So I took it back. However, I just wanted out of the engagement. I wanted Dick. Finally, I handed the unwanted ring to my mother and told her to give it back to my boy friend. He told me he was going to make Dick Hain wish he'd never been born. Eventually my dad disposed of the ring and recovered some of his lost investment when he sold it to one of his customers in our store. My boyfriend's family had been regular customers, and after the broken engagement, they quit trading at our store.

1952 at Duck Lake

My used car had acquired an alarming number of miles that summer while my boyfriend had driven it eighty miles each day to and from Muskegon to work, so my parents bought me a new 1952 Plymouth to commute between Mears and Central Michigan College.

My little brother, nine-year-old Terry expressed strong disapproval of my new boyfriend. Terry very much admired my muscular, athletic former boyfriend. The first time Dick and I appeared in public together holding hands, my little brother glared his distaste from across the street in Shelby where I was to tap dance for the Shelby Homecoming Celebration.

Here's what Terry wrote for our Golden Anniversary Celebration: "...I guess the memory of Bonnie and Dick that stands out the most is the first time I saw them together. Before we go there though, we need a little background. Bonnie went with a certain guy as long as I can remember. He was a star athlete at Hart, and was the one responsible for my interest in sports, and very much my hero. Being 9 or 10 years old, I really knew nothing about Bonnie's love life, or that she had broken up with my hero. So here we are going to the Shelby Homecoming. (I think Bonnie was tap dancing that night. I'm not really sure). Here I am walking with my mother, and behold across the street I see my sister walking with some guy, and it WASN'T my hero. It was some 6-3", 135 pound guy who I was sure had never played football or basketball in his life. My emotions went from mad, betrayed, to jealous....I have to say his standing improved a lot when he brought one of Purdue's star boxers home and introduced me, and also when I got to go to Purdue and see the great Len Dawson play. So you see, Dick did improve in my eyes; it just took awhile. And he did turn out to be the best brother-in-law I could have hoped for."

Dick had been short and thin till he grew to be six feet, two inches tall during his last year of high school. He's been thin and stayed thin all his life.

A year at junior college followed by a year at Purdue University had transformed him into a "man of the world" in the eyes of this inexperienced eighteen-year-old from Mears, Michigan (population 300) which my father often referred to as "the hub of the world." Mears had certainly been the hub of MY world till August, 1952, when Dick Hain turned my tiny world upside down.

My little sister Connie fell for Dick as quickly as I had. Here's the memory she shared at our Golden Anniversary Celebration: "I remember when Bonnie brought Dick to our house. I was about 6-1/2 years old and was infatuated with Dick. I went out of my way to keep his attention focused on me. Dick and I played games for hours...one in particular that sticks in my mind was a board game called "Pollyanna," which I still have! When I would tire of that, I would just sit on his lap, have conversation, and flirt!"

Summer ended and three hundred miles separated me at Central Michigan College from Dick at Purdue University. Our long-distance courtship commenced through letter-writing. I wrote to him three times a day, and he wrote to me three times a week. Our old letters are stored in the basement of our house.

I drove my new 1952 Plymouth to Purdue for the Military Ball and again for the Christmas Ball at Dick's fraternity house. He hitchhiked home to see me several weekends.

CMCE ROTC Kaydette

We were a Divine Set-up, though neither of us had yet made the acquaintance of the Ancient Divine Matchmaker. Within a very short while all the 1940's and 1950's love songs seemed to be written just for us. Each love letter we wrote had a line or two from a particular love song that seemed to express exactly what each of us was feeling when we wrote each letter. Our theme song was (and still is) "The Object of My Affection." Just for fun we sang it as a duet at our Golden Anniversary Celebration in 2004.

Since we've become grandparents, it has become part of our precious family lore to point to Aunt Ruth's dock and exclaim to our five grandchildren, "If that dock hadn't been there, YOU wouldn't be here!"

WEDDING, HONEYMOON

Mother of the Bride

Honeymoon

August 28, 1954, two years after Dick and I had fallen in love, we were married in a picture-perfect wedding in the Mears Church.

The Mears Methodist Church Ladies' Aid Society gave me a wedding shower and presented me with a starter set of Revere Ware. They served ice-cream and wedding cake at the wedding reception held in the front yard of my parents' new ranch-style house.

Even though neither Dick nor I really knew the Lord personally at that time, we now know that the Lord brought us together and kept us together. Nowadays when we pray out loud together, Dick often thanks God for bringing us together and keeping us together.

We honeymooned in a tent in the Upper Peninsula of Michigan. I woke up the morning after our wedding and discovered that I had my period.

Halfway through our honeymoon week I missed my mama so much that we left Copper Harbor and caught the car ferry to Ludington and returned home to visit Mama before we drove 300 miles to Purdue University for Dick's last semester before he'd graduate as a civil engineer.

It would be another thirteen years before we would be born again and begin to know God personally.

Here's something Dick wrote and read aloud to me in 2011 as an assignment from Counselor Bernadette during one of my recurring seasons of depression and despair:

"THINGS I LOVE ABOUT BONNIE."

When we first met I was awed by your beauty, smile, and friendliness. You were so exciting to be with. You also had a beautiful tan and figure. Of course you were in a bathing suit at the time. I was smitten to say the least!

As I got to know you I was impressed that you were very intelligent (Salutatorian of your High school class), talented, and ambitious (Miss Oceana Country, piano, tap dancing, cooking and scholarships to CMCE). On our first dates I was more than smitten and fell head over heels in love with you. We went to dances and it was so exciting introducing you to Big Band Music, and you followed my leading as if we had had lessons. You were so great to hold. Wow! You had so much energy. Those were the days.

It was so much fun to get to know you as we dated, wrote letters, visited each other at our colleges, and shared our summers in Michigan. Then we planned a wedding. I had no doubt that you were made for me and I for you. We started out our marriage at Purdue, living in a garage-size apartment on an alley. You made sure it was nice inside, and that I did my homework. You were a good cook and baker and we made it on less than $150 per month. Except my tuition was paid up by my folks. We also got a cocker spaniel puppy to complete our family. I was impressed that you took classes toward your degree in Education while we were at Purdue. After Purdue we spent *two years in the army. It included separation and life on a military base. It was not easy, but we stuck it out. You have always dressed well, kept your beauty and enthusiasm, been so clean. I was also impressed at your talent for keeping a neat house, and you were a good seamstress. I remember that I said you could have any thing that you wanted if you sewed it. After we had our first two boys you even sewed suits for them. You are so talented.*

I was so thrilled last week at the UBS Christmas Party when I talked to a couple of people there and the first thing they asked me was "Is your wife here?" They left me right away and went to where I showed them you were because they had enjoyed talking to you last year at the party. You are so good at meeting strangers and are excellent at keeping a conversation going.; At that moment you were talking with a Helen who you had just met and you both sounded like you had been friends forever. I love that about you!

I am still so attracted to you. I treasure our marriage with our special times of walking and cross-country skiing in the woods, traveling in the motor home, enjoying Duck Lake, making improvements to our home, cuddling at night, soaking in the hot tub together, eating out, going to church, viewing sunsets on Lake Michigan, et al...

I am especially impressed with your expertise of the English language. When I read to you, you not only know the correct pronunciation, but if I use the wrong word, you know what the word should be, and if I ask you what a word means, you usually have a good definition!

Chapter 3

PARENTING YEARS

$\mathcal{O}$ur first son arrived as a happy surprise. We'd been married three years. College and military obligations were behind us. We had moved our house trailer from Fort Leonard Wood, Missouri, back to Michigan and parked it in Pioneer County Park on Lake Michigan. I had landed a teaching job in a one-room school serving as a temporary classroom for fifteen first-graders and fifteen second-graders.

Morning sickness arrived as an uncomfortable surprise. A consultation with Dr. Cecelia S. Kay confirmed our suspicions that parenthood was just around the corner for us.

Teachers were in short supply in 1957. Dick's mom had just retired from twenty-three years teaching elementary school. She agreed to finish out the school year for me if that should be necessary.

The mothers of my Maple Ridge School students staged a surprise baby shower for me toward the end of the school year. They put a lace tablecloth on my desk and brought gifts and refreshments that we enjoyed while the children played outside in the school playground.

Our baby was due June 3. My mother-in-law went with me to hand out final report cards June 5. That afternoon I entered Hackley Hospital and William Christopher Hain ("Chris") arrived during the wee hours of June 6. When he was thirteen days old we packed our belongings, boarded the Ludington car ferry with my mother and little sister accompanying us, and moved to Milwaukee where Dick had a job and we had a brand new upstairs flat awaiting our arrival.

Motherhood was a "snap" after teaching school. I could nap while Chris napped. I could dress him up and take him outside for walks. He was my doll-baby, my very good baby. He slept all night when he was five weeks old. Aha! I had found my niche! If one baby was good, more babies would be even better. If I were home with one baby, I might as well be home with more babies. They could keep each other company and grow up to be each other's best friends as Dick and his sister were best friends and only fifteen months apart in age.

Within nine months I was expecting our second baby, and we felt very happy and excited about it. Dick would have loved a big family. He and his sister and their mother are just naturally good with children.

I discovered to my dismay that I am not good with toddlers. Suddenly there were twice as many little toenails and fingernails to clip each week. Suddenly there were two little boys keeping each other awake at night and during nap times. Days and nights were spent feeding babies and changing diapers. Those were the days before disposable diapers.

Chris & Ricky

Things had been getting steadily worse for me. I felt overwhelmed with responsibilities that severely challenged my emotional immaturity. Two babies in bottles and diapers wore me out.

I had taken amphetamines (aka "speed") during my second pregnancy. My ob-gyn doctor had given me free samples. They were the new "miracle drug" for weight loss and energy. They had been developed during World War II to enable military personnel to fight and function in the field without sleep or food.

My second son didn't sleep all night the first year of his life. His crib shared a bedroom with his brother's crib. Both babies cried each night. I cried too. I was very, very tired. Recently my second son remarked in a friendly way, "Well, Mom, maybe I would have slept better if you hadn't been on "speed" while you were pregnant for me." Good insight, son!

My emotional immaturity surfaced like an ugly scum on boiled milk. I tried very hard to be a good mother. I sewed matching outfits for our little boys. I took apart maternity clothes and refashioned them into little jackets for them. I was in deep waters. I was in over my head.

Dick did everything he could to ease the burden I felt. He came home every noon hour and gave them their bottles and played with them. He was so proud of his family.

I felt slighted when so much of his attention went to the children instead of to me. My inner child of the past was pounding on the box she'd been crammed into when I was about seven years old and my well-meaning mama had done her best to make me into the little girl she thought I should be...the little girl she herself had wanted to be...the little girl she vicariously lived through. With all the best intentions in the world, Mama had waited on me, indulged me, and spoiled me. Mama often described me as "such a bold little girl." She wanted me to be a "lady."

Neither of my parents had had the benefit of structured parental discipline during their formative years. They could not give me what they did not have. They gave me the best of what they did have to give, and I am thankful for the gift of always knowing I was wanted, cared for, and provided for. Counselor Bernadette helped me understand the underlying dynamics of my inner battles to be myself and not who or what someone else thought I had ought to be. She had me bring in a picture of myself taken when I was seven years old.

Me Age Seven

Dick helped me find just the right picture in Mother's photo album. "Honey! Come look at this!" Dick had put the old black and white snapshot onto the screen of our computer where it revealed a grinning little girl with arms distorted from having moved while the camera was clicking. Hands on hips, she is posing as she wants to pose instead of as she's supposed to pose.

In those days you did not waste film, and pictures were taken with considerable forethought. Mama was distressed by my bold move. She let me know how unhappy she was about it, and I never did like that picture of myself.

When Counselor Bernadette saw the enlarged print-out of seven-year-old Bonnie, she delightedly exclaimed, "This is the real you! This is the Bonnie who was put in a box, and sometimes she pounds on the box and makes noises." Bernadette asked me to frame the enlarged picture and keep it on display where I would be reminded of my true personality.

In retrospect, I see myself as that seven-year-old child competing with two babies in bottles and diapers for my husband's benevolent attentions. I'd been emotionally challenged to care for the unending demands of the invisible seven-year-old inside me and two babies crying for attention all day and all night.

One of my doctors always had me sit at his desk after he'd examined me and invited me to ask him any questions I might have. Year after year he listened sympathetically to my complaints. I felt for him the familiar awe of a patient with a respected physician. I was hungry for attention and affection that was in scarce supply at home.

One day after a regularly scheduled exam, I moved toward him and kissed him right on the mouth. The next day my phone rang. It was the doctor. "You bothered the hell out of me yesterday." Thus began his regular visits to our flat after he had finished his morning rounds at a nearby hospital. Thus began an infatuation that lasted most of the rest of my life.

I felt that I couldn't live without him and I knew I couldn't live with him. My conscience drove me crazy. My needs drove me to continue the affair. There seemed to be no escape. I knew I was neither a good wife nor a good mother. I knew that Dick was an excellent father. I wanted a divorce but there was no way I could support myself. There was barely enough money for one household. How could there possibly be enough for two? I felt like a failure, and I wanted to run away. But there was no place to run away to.

I would take the boys to Michigan and dump them with the grandparents and return to the peace and quiet of a child-free home. I felt absolutely helpless to escape the downward destructive path I'd embarked upon. I had a nervous breakdown.

Chapter 4

CHURCH

Our first two sons had arrived eighteen months apart in 1958 and 1959. It seemed important to find a church to get them properly baptized.

We had dropped out of church while we were in college. We hadn't gone to church during the two years Dick served his requisite two years in the military during the Korean Conflict.

Our only church experience had been Methodist, so in Milwaukee we searched for a Methodist church in a city of mostly Catholic and Lutheran churches.

We joined the one Methodist Church we finally found. Our sons got baptized. We got involved in a young couples group at church. Since I felt unsure of what I believed about God, I volunteered to teach third grade Sunday School. I learn best while I'm teaching.

I was instructed not to use the old chorus's we used to sing in the Mears Methodist Church: "The B-I-B-L-E, Yes That's the Book for Me, I stand alone on the Word of God, the B-I-B-L-E," "Jesus Loves Me This I Know, For the Bible Tells Me So," "One Door and Only One and Yet Its Sides Are Two. I'm on the Inside. On Which Side Are You?" "Climb, Climb Up Sunshine Mountain. Heavenly Breezes Blow," "This Little Light of Mine, I'm gonna' let it shine!,"etc. because they would just confuse the children.

It wasn't called "Sunday School" anymore. It was "Church School."

We hosted teachers from many different religions, and their beliefs seemed more solid than any I'd ever embraced. It didn't seem to matter what we believed. The Bible was not taken seriously. The preaching bored me. We decided that if that was all there was to it, it wasn't worth getting up on Sunday mornings and driving across town to go to church. We quit going to church.

HYMNS IN THE HALL

We lived in a two-bedroom downstairs flat in a beautiful old duplex on the corner of 48th and Auer in Milwaukee. A new couple moved in upstairs, and when I went into the hallway, I heard the old hymns coming down the stairs. I was surprised that anyone was still playing old hymns in that modern day and age.

I was especially surprised that the lady upstairs was very stylish and attractive and wore make-up. I'd come to believe that "real" Christians were mostly old and maybe handicapped so there was nothing better for them to do with their lives. In my mind "real" Christians definitely did NOT wear make-up or dress stylishly. There had been two or three outstanding "real" Christians in the Mears Methodist Church. One was old. One was crippled and walked with two crutches. None wore make-up. None dressed stylishly. None drank, danced, smoked or went to movies, and all frowned upon those who did drink, dance, smoke or go to movies.

The hymn-playing lady upstairs was Gloria. Her grandmother had built the duplex we rented. Gloria's uncle was our landlord. Gloria's husband was an ordained Pentecostal preacher.

One day Gloria looked right at me and declared, "Bonnie, there's more to being a Christian than speaking in tongues!" I hadn't a clue what she was talking about. When I had memorized 1 Corinthians 13 in Sunday School in Mears, I had had no idea what "speaking in tongues" meant. It hadn't even crossed my mind to wonder about it at all. I guess it had just come across to me as a poetic expression typical of Bible language.

Gloria's husband had recently left the ministry and graduated from the University of Wisconsin with a degree that qualified him to become principal of a school in Shorewood. Gloria had not enjoyed being the wife of a pastor of a church where make-up was frowned upon. She told me confidentially that she'd always worn everything but lipstick anyway.

Gloria was one amazing lady! She sang. She sewed. She spoke for women's groups. Woman's Day magazine featured her in three issues of their magazine. She was drop-dead good-looking. While she lived upstairs from us, she opened her arms and heart to me. She styled my hair. She listened to me and sat me down in a chair, put her hands on my shoulders and prayed out loud for me. She helped when I needed someone to keep an eye on our two little boys. Now she's in her 80's and she's still going strong.

One most memorable and special gift from Gloria was her gift of praying out loud for me. When she sat me down in a chair. stood behind me, placed her hands on my shoulders and prayed out loud for me, I curled my toes at the strangeness of it while my heart flushed with fresh hope that God actually existed and might even reach out of His heaven and help me in my dark pit of hopelessness and guilt.

There's something very special about having someone pray out loud for you. There's something healing in the gift of touch. I think of Gloria and thank God for her every time I sit someone down, place my hands on their shoulders and pray out loud for them and thus pass her prayer gift on to other people.

Gloria and her husband had gone church-shopping and discovered a new little Baptist church in the suburbs sprouting up west of Milwaukee. Gloria gave me a booklet "All the Days of My Life" written by the Baptist pastor. She told me I could call him if I ever needed to talk with someone about the emotional turmoil raging in my life. He had gone through emotional problems and would be available to help me with mine.

Chapter 5

HITTING BOTTOM

I felt homesick for the God of my childhood. I felt overwhelmed by the care of two babies in bottles and diapers. I felt disappointed in marriage. As I approached my 29th birthday, I felt more and more depressed and less and less glad to be alive. I wanted not to FEEL anymore. Increasingly, I entertained thoughts of suicide. But I didn't want it to hurt, and I didn't want to maim myself and survive. "I wish I was dead. I wish I was dead." Over and over those words went through my thoughts. Dick didn't know what to do. Neither did I.

PEACE, PEACE, WONDERFUL PEACE

The old hymn "Peace, peace, wonderful peace...coming down from the Father above, sweep over my spirit forever, I pray, in fathomless billows of love.

Ha! If only there were such peace...REALLY such peace.

Did whoever wrote that hymn know what it was all about?

Those old hymns from when I was a kid...they always puzzled me, I liked them...was fascinated by them...but was it possible that what they talked about really happened to real people? People who sang those hymns in church didn't seem different from people who didn't. I wished I could meet someone who REALLY knew what those hymns were talking about. I wished there was someone with real answers to all the things that never made sense about God and churches and the Bible.

ADULTERY

My romantic fantasies of marriage and "happily ever aftering" were fading fast. I was having an affair. My conscience was driving me crazy. I was in over my head and there seemed to be no way out.

I had become infatuated with a kindly older man in a position of trusted authority. Popular songs of the day described it well: "Falling in love again. Never wanted to. What am I to do? I can't help it." "Can't help falling in love with you." "One has my name. The other has my heart." On and on. Nothing new under the sun. But it was very new to me and totally "anti" all I'd wholeheartedly believed.

In the 1950's violins played when you kissed the "right one," and they "lived happily ever after." You knew it was the "right one" when those crazy wonderful feelings overwhelmed you. All this had happened when I'd met Dick in 1952. How could I be feeling like this about another man? I'd never doubted that Dick was THE ONE for me. How could I be overwhelmed by such intense "in love" feelings for another man? It made no sense within the framework of my beliefs.

Unfortunately, the attraction was mutual and doubly dangerous and distressing. One-sided "crushes" tend to die out from lack of fuel to sustain them. I'd had several such experiences. They had blossomed like acne on a teen-ager's face whenever someone (male or female) seemed to be meeting my buried baggage of needs. I'd "light up" in the presence of such a one. I'd obsess to distraction, longing to be with the current object of my attraction. The Bible calls it "inordinate affection" and advises us to avoid it. Eventually my zingy feelings would fizzle until the next infatuation came along.

Mother often complained, "You wear your heart on your sleeve." But I couldn't help it. All my life I just kept bumping along from one hero to the next one...male or female. "How our heroes lose their luster." At least mine did.

BLESSED NEEDINESS

However, in recent years I have begun to recognize and appreciate the peculiar blessing of the "blessed needy" with the blessed neediness of inner emptiness and desperate ceaseless craving for more, so much more. We empty ones possess an especially enormous empty space for the Holy Spirit to enter in, inhabit, and fill us with the Bread of Heaven that satisfies our blessed hunger. Matthew, chapter 5, reminds us of the peculiar privilege of felt spiritual poverty: "how blessed are the poor in Spirit, for they shall be filled!" Filled with what? Filled with the satisfying fullness that is only available to those who are empty enough and hungry enough to open our spiritual mouths wide and let Him fill us full and overflowing with the sweet, pure goodness of heaven-sent nourishment.

My intense inner neediness provides above-average emptiness for the Holy Spirit to inhabit and satisfy inordinate affections that otherwise seek fulfillment in human connections innately incapable of satisfying. Finite people cannot possibly meet and satisfy all the needs of other people. Only God can do that. He made us for Himself, and our hungry souls only find fulfillment in Him.

My prayer has become, "Lord Jesus, take my emptiness and fill it with adoration for You. Let me be totally infatuated (in love) with You. I offer my needy emptiness to You for You to fill and overflow to others. Let me glow with love for you so that others are drawn to the Christ who is alive in me."

Here's how I've come to understand adulterous affairs: mutual attractions possess a life of their own like gasoline poured upon a blaze. Red coals of old fires can and often do survive decades of neglect when unchallenged by the harsh realities of commitment or discovery.

Affairs are only beautiful to passion-blinded participants. They are ugly to everyone else.

There's something amiss when a great "love" must be kept secret. The excitement of "sneaking around" feeds the flame for awhile, but every lie leads to more lies until (like cancer) the truth succumbs to the lies feeding upon it, and the liar loses all credibility.

How sweet it is nowadays to have nothing to hide and no lies to cover with more lies!

ADDICTIONS AND IDOLS

Once tasted, forbidden fruit whets the appetite for more. Infatuation is dangerously addictive. It feels so good. But it never lasts. The zingy feelings of infatuation leave behind a feeling of letdown and longing for more. Like any addiction, it requires more and more to regain the original "high"

How foolish to abandon one's family and commitments to pursue feelings that cannot last!

Each of us has our own custom combination of personal addictions. The Bible calls them "idols." I read somewhere a long time ago that what we really worship is whatever it is that our thoughts automatically turn to when we are free to think our own thoughts. For some it's gossip, gluttony, alcohol, nicotine, prescription drugs, illegal drugs, shopping, watching TV, gambling, shoplifting, pornography, adultery, etc. We pursue an endless parade of idols. Every addiction requires more and more for the imbiber to obtain the original satisfaction.

Like fish after bait, we bite the hook and are caught and consumed by the Enemy of Souls. I was hooked on the emotional ecstasies of infatuation.

INFATUATION

In 1963 I had not yet learned the unhappy fact that what we call "being in love" is actually infatuation. Infatuation is temporary insanity. The cure is marriage. It's nature's way of propagating the race. One's capacity for infatuation is directly related to one's inner neediness. The greater the neediness, the greater one's capacity for the heady feelings of infatuation, because it feels as though this new object of one's infatuation is meeting all of those nagging inner needs that had been fostering an unpleasant sense of incompleteness and loneliness.

One really good thing about infatuation is that opposites tend to attract, and for a marriage to function well, it's good to have the whole realm of capabilities combined within one commitment.

The bad thing about opposites attracting is that the differences that attracted two people become the differences that make them incompatible later. Dick and I are definitely very different from each other, and those differences fueled my discontent. In all honesty, though, I cannot imagine the awfulness of being married to someone like me!

PSYCHIATRIC WARD

In April, 1965 I had an official nervous breakdown. The criterion for an OFFICIAL nervous breakdown is that you have to have been hospitalized for it. If you do it all at home, it doesn't count.

I truly believe that my first psychiatrist was sicker than I'll ever be...sort of like a lot of speech therapists have a serious speech impediment. I don't remember much about my second psychiatrist, except his name. My third psychiatrist eventually committed suicide. A 1980's survey identified the three highest stress groups in the nation as: dentists, psychiatrists, and mothers of pre-schoolers. I was the mother of two pre-schoolers.

Because I was suicidal, I spent six weeks in the locked ward of the psychiatric wing of the hospital where my second son had been born.

I had electric shock treatments that knocked me out, calmed me down, destroyed portions of my memory, and caused me to have "charley horses" (leg cramps) for the next several years.

I wanted to be well. I was determined to cooperate fully with the psychiatrist assigned to me. I would tell him all the truth and nothing but the truth.

However, the psychiatrist didn't believe me!

He refused to believe that my affair involved a respected doctor on the staff of that hospital.

Eventually I lied so I could escape from that place. I told the psychiatrist what he wanted to hear: that I had made up the story about having an affair with the doctor. Then I was released from the hospital and went back home.

The affair continued. I couldn't quit. I couldn't continue. My guilt intensified. Pain outweighed illicit pleasure. I craved escape. My suicide attempts became more frequent.

"I wish I was dead. I wish I was dead. I wish I was dead." Not very pretty grammar. Not very pretty sentiments. Defiant, rebellious, rampaging...venting overwhelming frustration, confusion, helplessness.

Quick, easy, sure way out. A way to run away and not hurt anymore. God is dead (if there ever was one). Jesus was a fairy tale. Heaven is when you're happy. Hell is when you're miserable. I've got all the Hell I can stand...and I want O-U-T! I just don't want to FEEL anymore! A new, sharp razor. All the pills I can find to swallow, a nice, warm bubble bath, a note, of course (I can't go on like this any longer), and oblivion! End of the line! Kind of exciting...easy...painless. Let the phone ring... doesn't matter...nothing matters anymore...

After two years of worsening conditions, my husband arrived home from work and found me unconscious in the bathtub.

DICK'S ACCOUNT OF WHAT HAPPENED NEXT

I felt confused, angry, overwhelmed and hopeless. I was sick and tired of how self-centered, mixed-up and suicidal Bonnie had become when she had two little boys who needed her to take care of them.

I changed out of my good clothes so I wouldn't get blood on them.

When I couldn't get her out of the bath tub myself, I went upstairs and got our neighbors to help.

Our two little boys had been playing around the corner at a neighbor's house. We immediately notified them that Bonnie was sick, and they said they would take care of the boys until I returned home from the hospital.

The police ambulance arrived and our boys watched from around the corner of our block as their mother was loaded into the ambulance.

Our upstairs neighbors said there was no need for me to rush to the hospital because I wouldn't be able to be with Bonnie anyway. They invited me to have supper with them.

They prayed with me and invited the Lord to take charge of the situation. I felt glimmerings of hope because of their faith in what God would do.

The police ambulance took me to the locked psychiatric ward of Milwaukee Country General Hospital.

When I woke up, I knew I had hit bottom. Shame and remorse overwhelmed me.

"Wash!"

What's she talking about, anyway?

"Wash!"

Where am I? In a tub! Not enough water...cold room...

"Wash!"

Somehow I washed...even my hair, in that unfriendly tub under that unfriendly gaze.

So hungry..of course...they pumped my stomach...

Then to bed...sleep...respite from reality...

But daylight must come. And it did.

Shame and hopelessness came too.

So hungry...weak and dizzy...

"Dress!"

But how? In that?

"Dress!"

That gray-white blouse? That faded skirt? I hate gathered skirts. I look terrible in them.

"Dress!"

"And brush your teeth...comb your hair."

Ugly things...flimsy...theirs...

Somehow I dressed, dazed...

No doors on the toilets!

What am I doing here? No place to run away...

Everything's gone...my clothes, make-up, privacy.

Let me out of here! I'm not crazy!

Nowhere to run to...no one listens...no one cares!

Standing in line...I can't eat that awful stuff...But I'm so hungry...

Isn't there anyone here I can talk to? Everyone's crazy.

Through the glass they look sometimes...

Do they think we're animals in a zoo?

Puddles! She's actually drooling puddles on the floor!

While she sits there pulling out her hairs one by one! She's half bald from it!

Why won't that one shut up? Screaming and yelling. Screaming and yelling.

Here's one...she looks more normal...let's play Scrabble...
So we ask the people behind the glass, and they give us Scrabble... and we try to play...try to concentrate...impossible...no use..forget it...

She says she shot herself...says she put herself in here on purpose... says she can't handle things at home. Could anyplace be worse than this place?

They say I've got to answer them...okay, I'll tell them everything... maybe they can help straighten me out...if only SOMEONE could help!

So many of them...and they're looking at me...I look awful...these clothes, no make-up, no hairdo, couldn't they even have toothbrushes that didn't bend in two when you use them?
They're asking me things.
They sound like they're making fun! I'm telling you the truth...I am!
They don't believe me! They're all against me! What can I say?
That's all for now.

Back to the big, noisy room where they watch us through windows.
She's still drooling puddles...still pulling out her hair...
that one is still yelling...
How can I "go" when there's no door on the toilet?

Blood test...I hate needles..oh well, what's the difference...
So much blood they're taking! Funny...nothing matters anymore...
Back to the big noisy room down the echoing hall so wide, so high.
I feel strange...my legs feel like rubber...think I'm going to faint.
Feels good. "Put your head down!"
Don't want to...this feels good...but nice things don't last...
Ugh..back again...dreadful place...no one cares...nothing matters...

Look down there! Out the window...down...far away...over there...
nurses marching with capes, caps, uniforms...respectable, normal...

heads held high...Graduation? Just look at them!

And look at me: ugly bandage on my wrist. Ugly clothes. Ugly hair. Ugly! If I can ever hold my head up again in public,

I'll never take that privilege for granted again.

"Line up!" Where? "Line up!" I can't eat this..."Well, leave it then..."

Visitors now...out there...in the hall...lots of them...there's Dick! What's he doing there? He's smiling at me! He looks so normal! Good to see him! Dick, can you get me out of here?

"Line up!" Why? Why bother? I can't eat this either...

"Line up! Hurry up! Over there!"

But I can't eat...never mind...I'll just take it and leave it...

Will this day never end?

Back in the big room where they sit behind glass and watch us... Turn off that television!

So loud...can't get away from it...even the toilets don't have doors.

The TV boomed mercilessly and constantly. I've never liked TV. I'd never seen Billy Graham on TV till my first full day of incarceration. It was his Hawaiian Crusade. There they were: HYMNS again! After the hymns Billy Graham preached a sermon, and there was no place for me to escape from hearing it.

What's he saying? might as well listen...

Says he never heard anyone say they were sorry

they'd invited Jesus to take over their lives

but he's heard plenty of people say they were sorry

they'd waited so long to do it.

He says it only takes a mustard-seed-size faith. Maybe I have that much.

Couldn't prove there was no God. Maybe there IS a God.

No way to prove there isn't.

God! If You're there, God, if you're there...from now on, God, I'm all yours, God, if you're there, and I don't care what you do with me.

46

I really don't care anymore. Nothing matters to me anymore.

I know it means one thing for sure will have to go (my affair). But so what?

I gave that up anyway when I used the pills and the razor.

Peace! I feel calm! Almost happy! I wonder what's going to happen. What time is it? Almost morning. All night I couldn't sleep...thinking, thinking, thinking thinking about God, thinking about what Billy Graham said.

Now I'm tired. Feels like I could sleep...

"There must have been some mistake.
But here are your clothes. Get dressed."

Where am I? What's happening? Morning! Already! What's she saying?

There's my clothes! My own clothes! I can have my own clothes!
How good they feel!
Feels so good to have my own clothes again...clothes that fit me.

Seems like heaven to wear things that look nice again~
And hand lotion~ Smells wonderful~

I've lost weight~ Everything fits looser.
That's ONE good thing out of all this mess.
Oh! I look so nice! After their ugly clothes...

"You're going home. There must be some mistake.
But they say you're going home.
No one leaves here in less than 2 weeks...
especially with a history like yours.

Here we go...through the big door...the heavy door...
the locked door...unlocked for me now.

There's Dick! What's going on? Am I REALLY going home?

Oh, thank God! Thanks God! I'll do anything, anything, anything at all to get things straightened out...to get ME straightened out.

I'll co-operate. Maybe there's a doctor...a psychiatrist, someone I can talk to and like...someone who will like me and help me if I REALLY co-operate.

I'm ready now. I'll do anything to get better. I really will...

DICK'S ACCOUNT OF HIS EXPERIENCE

At about that same time, for some reason, I began to have a positive feeling that this was a turning point in our lives. I almost felt like something miraculous was happening. Maybe things were going to work out after all. I had not informed any of our family in Michigan what had happened.

I was led to people who gave me advice about what actions I should take.

I found out about Milwaukee Sanitarium and that they had an opening available.

When I asked people at the hospital if I could take Bonnie home, they said they had to release her if I requested it. So by late Friday afternoon I went to the hospital and picked her up and took her home. As it turned out, Bonnie never had to go to Milwaukee Sanitarium.

As soon as we returned home to our rented flat, I searched until I found the booklet that Gloria had given me.

I'm home! I'm really home! I can use the phone and call anyone I like. There's no one here I have to ask. There are drapes! And carpeting! Didn't know I'd missed them till I went without them. Maybe someday I can go back to that awful place and take those poor people some nice hand lotion and some pretty things.

Anything it takes, I'll do. I'll co-operate. I'll really try. It's not easy to flush pills away down the toilet. Diet pills, sleeping pills, hidden pills... all down the toilet. I love those pills. Must throw away reminders of my wrong ways...pictures, letters, cards...into the fire of the fireplace. 'Dear old fireplace...place of comfort, of warmth, of dancing flame, source of solace when outer darkness joins my inner dark. Into the fire for good go pictures, letters, cards, souvenirs...things I wrongly love.

Next: take a bath...nice, long bubble bath...relax, rest, soak up its perfume, cleanse all my hidden parts, clean for my new start. I wonder if it will work this time.

If this doesn't work, there's no place else to go.
I knew better, and I did all those things anyway.
It's not like I didn't know better.
I KNEW I shouldn't be doing what I was doing,
if there really was a God.
But what's the difference what I do...
if there's no God?
I did what I wanted to do BECAUSE I wanted to
when I decided there was no God.

The only thing that mattered was to be happy.
I was happy...crazy happy...sometimes...
There was something to live for...
something to get out of bed for...something I WANTED to do...
Oh, I was SO happy!
Like when I was 18 before I was married,
before 2 babies in bottles and diapers never let me sleep,
and I got so tired...
and there was no money
and nothing to look forward to
except being tired with never enough money
and too much to do so it never got done
and I got so tired...couldn't cope.
Crying babies...wanted to run away...nowhere to go.
My conscience driving me crazy.

Gloria often said I could talk to her pastor.
But what if I couldn't relate to him?
Those psychiatrists were creeps.
I feel foolish calling someone I don't even know.

Dial his number.
Says he'll be right out.
Funny, he doesn't even know me.

Dick, Will you take the boys to the park or somewhere so I can talk with this pastor of Gloria's when he gets here?

Although I didn't know it at the time, Dick had already prayed with Gloria and her husband upstairs the night the police ambulance took me to County Hospital. With help from Gloria and her husband, Dick had given me to God. So Dick was ready for me to talk to this pastor of theirs. Dick was ready to try ANYTHING that might help me. Psychiatrists hadn't helped. Pills hadn't helped. Hospitals hadn't helped. Dick was ready to try anything that might help me. He and our two little boys left. I was alone by the front window, watching, waiting..

Chapter 6

BORN AGAIN

The time for me to be born again had arrived at last. My Heavenly Father had arranged for home delivery assisted by Gloria's Baptist pastor.

I didn't want Dick to know what I was doing until I found out if it would work this time. I had never known anyone who had experienced life-altering changes after they'd prayed the sinner's prayer.

Before my parents had met, they had each gone forward during altar calls at church meetings, and it hadn't worked for either of them. Because nothing had changed for them, they had expressly forbidden me to ever "go up in front and make a fool of myself." Sometimes when there had been altar calls at churches, I had felt like I had to grab hold of the seat of my chair and force myself not to go forward during altar calls.

Dick was a desperate man and willing to do anything it took. He left me home alone while he and our little boys went to visit the Milwaukee zoo under construction west of the city.

I was a self-centered package of neediness all wrapped up in myself, incapable of caring about my husband or our two little sons.

I stood by the front window, watching and waiting for the stranger to appear. A vintage black Cadillac with fins pulled up and parked in front of our flat. A tall, good-looking man emerged from the car and walked to our front door. I'm prejudiced in favor of tall men. He had a "butch" haircut. In 1965 I adored "butch" haircuts. I had never seen a pastor with a "butch" haircut. This stranger looked nice and normal. I liked his looks. I opened the door and wondered what would happen next.

I had tried God so many times and it had never worked for me. I felt like this was my last chance to try again.

Because of my affair, my suicide attempts, and my failure as a mother, I felt like I had out-sinned any hope there might have been for me with God. I knew just enough about God to feel hopelessly guilty about my sin. But I did not have a clue as to how God (IF there really was a God) could make a difference in my life. I could not see how the crucifixion of Jesus thousands of years ago, thousands of miles away from where I lived could make any difference in what was happening in my life in the 1960's. I had tried reading my Bible, but it hadn't made any real sense to me. I'd been bored beyond tolerance in church.

I wasn't even sure there WAS a God. Once I had said something to Gloria about, "IF there's a God..." and she had looked me straight in the face and said firmly and confidently, "There's a God, Bonnie." She was so darn SURE! I would have given anything to have been that sure about God.

Pastor Bob made himself comfortable in our living room and asked me to tell him about myself. I told him the truth, the whole truth, and nothing but the truth. The man was shockproof! He didn't flinch. He just sat there and smiled confidently. He seemed to know a lot of answers for all my questions. He was so SURE there was a God....a God who still cared about me...a God who wanted to give me a fresh start... like wiping a chalkboard clean and starting over with a clean slate. It seemed too good to be true, but it was sure worth a try. I'd do anything to make it work. I'd quit anything I needed to quit.

While I was still wondering what was coming next, Pastor Bob asked me if I would be willing to say a little prayer with him. He would say the words, and I would repeat them after him. I would have stood on my head and recited the alphabet backward if he'd asked me to. Of course I would pray his prayer with him.

It was the same old sinner's prayer thanking Jesus for dying on the cross for my sin, and then inviting Jesus Christ to come into my heart and take over everything in my life. I'd prayed it more times than I could remember. I've never had a problem admitting that I'm a sinner. It has always been so obvious, a very apparent fact of life. I've never understood why people have a problem accepting the doctrine of "original sin." You never have to teach a child how to sin. Pastor Bob seemed to expect the old sinners' prayer to have some good positive outcomes this time. I certainly hoped he was right. But I wasn't going to tell anyone about it until I was sure it had worked.

He asked me if I had a Bible. I knew I had a Bible somewhere. I looked around until I found it and brought it to him. He opened it like he really knew his way around a Bible. He read out loud to me from 2 Chronicles 16:9...The eyes of the Lord roam to and fro throughout the whole earth to show Himself strong in behalf of them whose heart is perfect toward Him.

I was impressed that this man knew so much about my Bible. I'd never encountered that verse in all my years of Sunday School and church. How had he known it was there?

Then he gave me an assignment: I should read the whole book of John. I said I would.

Dick arrived home with our sons, and it was time for the pastor to go home and we would find out if this had worked. I waited for him to head toward the door, but he just stood there and chatted with Dick.

I was horrified and embarrassed when he said, "Dick, your wife just invited Christ into her life. Would you like to invite Christ into your life too?"

Dick was shocked and speechless. He didn't understand. He didn't need more religion. I'm the one who's a mess. Dick just stood there looking around.

Finally he pointed at me and said, "She's sick. Not me." And that was the truth.

DICK'S PERSPECTIVE HERE

In the first place, I didn't understand what he was offering. I suppose I had a misconception of what Christianity was really about. I felt prejudiced against Baptists, born-againers, and holy-rollers. I was willing for whatever it took for Bonnie to get straightened out, but I didn't think I needed to change. A few months later I discovered I could have a personal relationship with Jesus Christ.

As Pastor Bob was leaving (finally! at last!) I whispered to him that he shouldn't talk to Dick about those things again.

Pastor Bob said he had just one thing to ask of Dick...would he bring me to his church just once? Even though it was such a long way for us to go...miles away in the western suburbs...farther than our old Methodist Church had been, Dick agreed to do so. I felt a wave of hope, and it felt very good.

Before Pastor Bob left, he invited us to come to a progressive dinner with people from his church.

HYMNS ON A SCHOOL BUS

We did go on that progressive dinner. I still had the bandage on my wrist from my most recent suicide attempt. I sat beside Dick in the school bus seat with my head down as the happy diners sang while the bus traveled all over greater Milwaukee for various courses of the most elaborate church dinner I'd ever witnessed. These Baptists were singing the same hymns, choruses, and songs I used to sing in the Mears Methodist Episcopal Church.

I tried to hide my bandaged wrist. I could not look anyone in the eyes. They were so NORMAL and I was such a mess. Those folks welcomed us with the warmest outreach we'd ever experienced anywhere before. We were complete strangers to them, and they acted like they loved us and considered us to be some of the most special, lovable people they'd ever met.

We were drawn as by a magnet to visit their church when they invited us.

At first Dick dragged his feet about that. He felt that if we had found the actual truth about God, we should go back to our Milwaukee Methodist Church and tell the people there what we'd found.

Dick thought we should go back to that church and give it another try. Maybe what had been wrong wasn't church, but me. Maybe now church would make sense and be interesting. We tried going back. But there was still no meaning. Everything was still so boring.

I begged Dick to let us go to Pastor Bob's church. And we became regular attenders at Pastor Bob's Baptist Church.

Dick wrote a letter to the pastor of our old Methodist church, explaining what we had found and why we were going to another church. I don't think he ever received a reply.

Several years later I ran into the pastor's wife in a store and told her how well things were going for us, and she said, "Oh Bonnie, I knew you'd get over it (doubts, depression, desperation) eventually."

GROWING IN GRACE

The week after the hospital week Pastor Bob again arrived at our front door. He said he'd come to see how things were going. He brought me a Bible...just a New Testament in a new version called "Amplified." He said I should read "John." Okay, I would read "John." Strange: he GAVE me that Bible! He seemed so sure something important was in it for me. He said to read "John." So I read "John."

"John" didn't make much sense to me. Too many impossible stories... stories I'd known as a child. Stories of miracles, demons, crazy stuff. When I'd heard those stories in Sunday School, my dad had told me they weren't true. They were like myths or fairy tales. Anyway, I read "John" in the new Bible from Pastor Bob.

I wondered, "Why is he so nice to me?"
"Why does he seem to care so much what happens to me?
He acts like he really knows me, like he understands me.
How come he's always so cheerful and smiles so much?
No matter what I say, he listens and acts interested.
No matter what I say, nothing seems to worry him.
He seems so normal.
After he leaves, I feel full of hope.
I don't understand any of this.
I don't really believe most of it.

But he seems so sure...like Gloria seemed so sure that there was a God, and that God really cares about everyone (even me) and wants to give fresh starts to people who want fresh starts. I hope they're right.

There's no place to go if they're wrong.

So I rode piggy-back on their beliefs for several years.

Sometimes my doubts dragged me down, drove me nearly crazy.

If this didn't work, I had no place else to go. It HAD to work!

Sometimes it made so much sense.

Sometimes it seemed like fairy tales again.

I wrote a lot of poems about how I felt. I showed them to Pastor Bob. He seemed interested in them.

He smiled after he read them and said it would be interesting to see how my poems would change as I changed.

He really seemed to think I was going to change! I sure hoped he was right.

But it seemed too good to be true

A CHRISTIAN HUSBAND

It had been June 10 , 1965, when I had stayed up all night in Milwaukee Country General Hospital and prayed, "If You're there God, I'm all Yours, and I don't care with You do with me." The following August Dick went with the Baptist men to an advance (not a "retreat") at the Green Lake Conference Center.

DICK'S ACCOUNT OF HIS TIME AT GREEN LAKE

I'd never been on a retreat ("advance") before. I very much enjoyed playing golf, studying and discussing the Bible, and joking around with this friendly bunch of men. This kind of Christian fellowship was new and very special to me. I'd never experienced anything like it before.

The idea of receiving Christ into my life was a new and unfamiliar concept to me.

During our last evening at the advance Pastor Bob presented the opportunity for us to invite Christ into our lives and to raise our hands to acknowledge that we had done so. I raised my hand because I really did want Christ in my life. I wasn't the only man in our group who did that.

I was anxious to get home to tell Bonnie what I had done.

Dick arrived home on August 28, our 11th anniversary. He said, "I've brought you an anniversary present. I've brought you a Christian husband."

HUNGER, APPETITE

Here's how I know I was born again: I was hungry for what the Bible calls "the milk of the word." Milk is easy to ingest and digest. Milk is food for babies. The harder things in the Bible are called "the meat of the word." (1 Corinthians 2:2, Hebrews 5:13, 1 Peter 2:2)

Newborn babies are hungry for milk. Suddenly the Bible became delicious and satisfying for my spiritual hunger.

I had a voracious appetite for more and more and more. I was greedy for more and more and more.

The Bible made sense as it had never made sense before.

Where there's life, there's hunger. The Bible says that those who hunger and thirst after righteousness are especially blessed, for they shall be filled.

We went to church three times a week: Sunday morning, Sunday evening, and Wednesday evening. Once a month I eagerly attended an evening women's Bible study on Song of Solomon. Sunday School women's group were studying 1 Corinthians.

The 14th verse in 1 Corinthians jumped out at me and explained to me the reason the Bible had never made sense to me before: "The natural man receiveth not the things of the Spirit. Indeed, he CANNOT. For they are spiritually discerned."

I had been a "natural man" (woman), born deaf and blind to the word of God. The Bible teaches that everyone is automatically born into the evil kingdom of Satan. Everyone is born into a fallen world order temporarily governed by the Father of Lies, caught in the clutches of the Evil Trinity: the world, the flesh, and the devil.

1 John 2:16 sums up the way of the "world" as "the lust of the flesh, the lust of the eyes, and the pride of life" which boils down to passion-possessions- position or sex-stuff-status. These three things motivate natural human behavior. It's not a popular message.

Until the Holy Spirit heals our spiritual deafness and blindness, we simply CANNOT see, hear, or comprehend Truth.

The Cross of Christ makes no sense at all to the natural man or woman. God's ways seem like foolishness to the natural man or woman.

Until we are reborn (born again) and the Holy Spirit makes the Bible make sense to us, we lack the capacity to grasp its timeless treasures.

Verse 27 in 1 Corinthians really jumped out at me and made me laugh. Here's why: When I was a child and did something that annoyed her, Mother used to say to me, "Bonnie, quit acting so foolish."

The verse in 1 Corinthians says: "God hath chosen the foolish!" Hey, that means ME!

WHAT MADE THE DIFFERENCE

I think the reason my invitation to invite Christ into my life "worked" this time involved two essential conditions that had been missing earlier in my life. This time I had no viable options. I had hit bottom and was so far down that I could only look up. Christ seemed to be my one and only hope left in this world. I knew I could not cope on my own. And this time there was plenty of wise, loving, faithful follow-through from mature believers ministering to this newborn believer.

Simply reciting words doesn't change people. Reciting wedding vows doesn't make a person married. It's whom you say them with and whom you go home and live with that makes the difference.

God doesn't have any grandchildren, and we all have to be individually born into His family as sons and daughters. Tradition cannot substitute for genuine relationship. Sitting in church doesn't make a person a Christian any more than sitting in a garage causes a person to become a car. Spiritual growth requires spiritual food. The Bible is God's food and drink for His children.

Pastor Bob preached through various books of the Bible Sunday morning and Sunday evening. I sat in the front row and could not get enough of it. I was SO hungry for this kind of Bible teaching. I'd never in my life heard anything so dynamic and meaningful.

One sermon in particular "hit" me when I heard it and remains in my memory as fresh as the day Pastor Bob preached from the Bible, beginning at verse in 2 Kings 19:14. King Hezekiah was facing an impossible situation. Hezekiah "spread it before the Lord," and God stepped in and saved the day. I wrote two poems about spreading everything before the Lord. It's the best way there is to cope with everything that life sends our way. Nothing is too difficult for God!

I survived between services by listening to Christian music at home. I played it LOUD to drown out the old way of thinking that lingered in my head.

I devoured my Amplified Bible as meaning leapt from the pages into my hungry soul.

I purchased audio cassettes of the Bible being read aloud. I listened to them as I worked around the house, as I napped, and as I went places in the car. I immersed myself in the Bible so I would know for myself what it said.

I hid God's word in my heart. That's what Scripture instructed me to do.

I wanted to know for myself what the Bible really said...not what the Methodists or Catholics or Lutherans or any other denominations said that it said.

Each time something made sense to me, I wrote a poem about it. Poems came out of me like I was pregnant for them. Three or four or more came pouring out onto paper every day. I showed them to Pastor Bob, and he suggested I write a poem based on the word "Discovery."

One day I was hanging laundry outside on the clothesline when the first two lines came to me: "Discovering daily who God really is. Thanking Him daily He's mine and I'm His." Pastor Bob had kept telling me to thank God, not to beg God. That seemed important to him.

I ran indoors and wrote them down and went back outside to finish hanging out the laundry. Then another two lines would come to me, and I'd run back indoors and write them down. I wrote as though I really believed, even though I still had plenty of doubts.

I'd never understood and had often wondered what grace really meant. It was a church word I'd heard a lot. I knew a girl named Grace. I knew ballet dancers should have grace. My ballet teacher let me know in no uncertain terms that I did not have grace.

Pastor Bob had answers for all my questions. He said that grace means a favor from God...a favor you don't earn or deserve, and you just accept it.

The Bible was beginning to make sense to me sometimes. I underlined where it did and showed it to Pastor Bob. He said that was God's way of speaking to me. He really seemed to believe that.

It simply amazed me that everyone at church seemed to believe the Bible was true and very important for people nowadays. Something in me was awfully hungry to understand everything about God and the Bible.

Chapter 7

AUTHOR

od was becoming more and more real to me, and life seemed exciting and full of hope. Pastor Bob's favorite Bible verse was: "Christ in you...Hope..." Maybe it WAS true! Maybe this WAS going to work for me!

Poems kept coming, almost like I was pregnant for them. So I wrote them down. I just sat down with pencil and paper, and poems happened. I "saw" things I'd never "seen" before. It was fun, fulfilling, exciting, and easy. Every day, more poems. Every day, more "seeing."

DISCOVERING DAILY

Discovering daily who God really is.
Thanking Him daily He's mine and I'm His.
Discovering daily God's great love for me...
Such mercy, forgiveness, amazingly free.

Discovering daily that God really cares.
Discovering daily He does answer prayers.
Discovering daily what grace really means:
Unmerited favor beyond all my dreams.

Discovering daily God speaking to me.
He speaks through the Bible. Once blind, now I see.

Discovering, discovering each day that I live
That all that I need, He freely will give.

Discovering daily Christ working through me,
Accomplishing daily what never could be.
Discovering daily I can't, but He can.
Thanking Him daily for my place in His plan.

Discovering daily how REAL life can be
When I'm living in Christ, and He's living in me.
Discovering daily a song in my heart
With anticipation for each day to start.

Delighting and basking in love so divine,
Secure in the knowledge I'm His and He's mine.
Besides mere contentment, excitement I see!
A daily adventure: Christ living in me!

Pastor Bob was well-pleased by that poem. He composed music for it and sang it in church. The music for the "Discovering" poem became the theme music for the church's daily radio broadcast called "DISCOVERY."

Major Ian Thomas, an English author, lecturer, and founder of Torchbearer Bible Schools, liked that poem and read it to groups of people all around the world.

The "Discovering" poem was printed on back of the church bulletins every Sunday. God must be answering my prayer to grow fast. I felt important, but I tried not to let it show. I kept having doubts and trying not to let them show. Years went by till my life really matched my poems. Hundreds of poems recorded my growing insights. Hundreds of weeks contained my confusion and carried my struggles to grow up into my poems.

A few months after I met Christ I met Win. She'd heard about my poems and my story. Her church was having a special dinner at the Jolly Troll restaurant. They wanted a speaker, so they invited me. Pastor Bob's wife Nina and Marge went with me. I wore a pink dress.

A gray-haired lady sat in the back of the crowd and nodded her head a lot. She seemed to like the things I said. Afterward we met in person. Win was someone very special. She became my spiritual mentor. For several years I called her every weekday morning at 8:00. She listened to me and answered my questions.

I watched her like a hawk. I'd never seen anyone live out the Christian life the way she did. To this day I recall incidents I was privy to in Win's personal life, and therein discover possibilities of handling similar circumstances in my own experience.

Win's faithful mentoring continues to be for me "the gift that keeps on giving." Thank you, Win! And thank you, Heavenly Father, for sharing Win's expertise with me.

LOVING THE LIMELIGHT

The church sponsored a 5-day-a-week 15-minute radio broadcast, and Pastor Bob read one of my poems almost every day.

People wrote to request copies of the poems.

We had a small paperback poem book printed. The first printing was for 5000 copies that sold for 75 cents apiece. A second book "Dimensions" was printed. Another 5000 copies. Then a second printing of "Discovery." Another 5000 copies.

PASTOR BOB'S FOREWORD TO MY POEM BOOKS

DISCOVERY

The telephone rang. I answered and listened for a moment and then reassured the person at the other end of the line (a stranger to me) that I would come at once. Arriving at the home of Mr. and Mrs. Richard Hain, I met Bonnie for the first time and heard her story of how unbearable life can be...unbearable to the point of an attempt to take her own life by means of slashing her wrists. As she related her black story...the the end nearly in sight...Jesus Christ, by her invitation, stepped into her life as Saviour and Lord.

Jesus Christ said He was the Vine and that we are the branches. Since this is true, we could expect Him to begin His flow of Life through her. In the process of this activity, His Life flowing through her, this book of poems has come into existence. Some of them were written before coming to really know Him. Most of them have been written since that day of Discovery.

So much has been written concerning the externalism of Christianity that these poems seem as a breath of fresh air when reading about the Indwelling and Triumphant Christ...working within and through an individual. I trust Him to use them in the lives of the many thousands of people that read them. Pastor Robert G. Hobson (1966)

DIMENSIONS

In the book of poems entitled "Discovery" it was mentioned in the foreword that because Jesus Christ is the Vine and we are the branches, we could expect Him as the Vine, to begin His flow of Life through us.

The poems in this book are a part of 'that flow' within and through the life of Bonnie Hain. Many of them have been written because of her discovery of the principles contained within them.

The privilege that belongs to everyone is to make the initial DISCOVERY of Jesus Christ. It is then the believer's God-given right to begin to discover the DIMENSIONS of Who Jesus Christ is.

What a tragedy when people make only the discovery of Jesus Christ as Saviour (as great as that is) without making further discoveries of the DIMENSIONS of Jesus Christ.

It is His Plan that the DIMENSIONS of His Peace, Joy and Trustworthiness become a Living Reality in the midst of pressure, stress and strain.

It is my confident trust in Him to take these principles described in this book and use them to broaden, lengthen, deepen and widen His DIMENSIONS in your life. Pastor Robert G. Hobson (1967)

Pastor Bob continued to compose music to some of my poems and sing them on the radio and in church. I was invited to share my testimony publicly, and the books were sold at those events.

I loved the limelight and the attention. Dick often introduced himself as "Mr. Bonnie Hain." He was proud of me. My boys were proud to be "Bonnie Hain's boys." What a change in such a short period of time!

My teaching career began to blossom as well. LBJ's Great Society had unleashed lavish public funds to facilitate remedial reading clinics. School superintendents were scrambling to hire certified remedial reading teachers to claim their share of the windfall. In September I was hired to direct a remedial reading clinic in a bedroom community north of Milwaukee. Unbelievable! From County General in June to directing a remedial reading clinic in September!

I prayed for each student as I drove to and from school each day, a half hour each way, and the children's test scores improved so significantly that our federal funds were doubled the second year! God and I were on a roll!

Chapter 8

CHURCHES

The little Baptist church had begun in 1958 with five families in an abandoned one-room school house where Milwaukee suburbs were developing.

When we began attending in 1965, the newly-built sanctuary seated 100 people. Attendance grew and the church building grew to accommodate the steady stream of new believers and renewed older believers attracted to the warmth and light of the work being accomplished by the Holy Spirit in that attractive setting.

By 1968 the expanded building was sold so a bigger one could be built in a new and more spacious location.

Skeptics declared that if Pastor Bob ever left, the church would fall apart. I sometimes wondered if my faith would fall apart if Pastor Bob ever left. In 1969 Pastor Bob left, and I discovered that I could continue growing spiritually without my hero in the the pulpit. A new chapter began for me.

In December, 1970 our new pastor, Stuart Briscoe, an itinerant preacher and associate of Pastor Bob's friend Major Ian Thomas, arrived from England. Our church entered another exciting era.

We rented a theater to house overflow crowds who came to hear our new pastor preach, and God lavished upon us the finest expository preaching of that day and age.

His gifted wife Jill taught Bible classes and enlisted budding speakers and teachers in our ever-expanding church family.

Youth ministries sprang into existence twice a week. Dick took our boys to church for those activities while I stayed home with Baby Bobby and hosted early-teen girls for weekly sessions of fun and fellowship.

Baby Bobby was born in 1969 and named after my two fathers: my spiritual father Robert and my physical father Keith: Robert Keith Hain. I had desperately wanted another baby to make up for my neglect of my first two babies. I wanted a chance to "do it right" this time. So what happened? I made the exact opposite mistakes from those I had made with the first two! I drowned him in attention, gave him everything he wanted, spoiled him, and weakened him by doing everything for him instead of stepping back and letting him learn for himself. He's still recovering from "smothering mothering."

Bonnie and Bobby

All three sons have generously forgiven and offered gracious appreciation for their childhoods in our family. Their grandparents deserve much credit for the stability that their involvement provided. All three sons are each other's best friends and consistently extend encouragement and affection to their slowly-maturing, still growing-up, emotionally unstable bipolar mother. According to Scriptural promises, God has restored the years the locusts have eaten.

Whenever the church doors were open during our Milwaukee years, we were there. We were in church several days a week, and it was wonderful. This was the way things were supposed to be! We had well-known Christians speaking in our church so our gifted pastor would speak in their churches. Our missions festivals were spiritual feasts.

Then the unthinkable happened.

COLORADO

We had to move across the country 1000 miles away from where everything was wonderful and everyone knew how wonderful I was.

We moved because Dick designed freeways and environmentalists had shut down freeway construction in Milwaukee. His employer wanted him to work in the Colorado office where business was booming. So we moved.

And soon everything that could be shaken was shaken.

I believed that if I "walked my talk" and a church remained faithful to Scripture, it didn't matter what denomination it was. But I felt like an outsider looking in when we joined a church near our home in Colorado.

Unfortunately, I found the preaching uninspiring and often boring. I took Vivarin to stay awake in church. I suppose I had been spoiled by the excellent preaching we'd enjoyed in Milwaukee. I have a very low tolerance for boredom.

Dick said that I should work in the nursery so someone who wanted to be in church could be there. I tried that, but I've never been good with babies and toddlers, and it got so bad that I started having headaches on Sundays. I increasingly dreaded church as I had dreaded it during my high school years while I'd been active in Sunday School. I've always loved Sunday School, but more often than not I've had a hard time staying awake during most sermons.

CHURCH POLITICS

Then church politics reared its ugly head and a group of people left the church when the youth pastor was fired. One Sunday morning there was no organist. He had left with group that began meeting in another church's building.

Not long after that we received an urgent phone call to attend a special meeting that was being hushed up. When we arrived, one of my favorite pastors was sitting, grief-stricken, in a chair, holding his bowed face with both hands. He was being dismissed.

His followers started having him speak at house churches to be formed as a result of this development.

The music pastor was fired. He was my favorite pastor on staff. He tearfully read his resignation letter that the senior pastor had written and instructed him to read out loud as though he had written it. Another segment of church folks exited our congregation.

A dear minister friend and his wife lost a much-wanted baby in "crib death." Soon after that, this minister was fired because he was too involved with an offshoot of the Charismatic movement.

About the same time that my church was splitting, one of my sons got a divorce. I got menopause. I got uninvited to speak to a women's group that had previously adored me.

The reason I was uninvited was a talk I'd been asked to give on "Stress." As usual, my lecture room was standing room only, and the women expressed a great deal of appreciation for my openness and honesty.

But a few women were offended by my graphic language. In particular, I opened my talk with a quote from Ann Landers: "Life is one damn thing after another." If I'd opened it with a quote from Scripture such as "In this life you shall have tribulations," it would have been okay.

I had sought to cushion the shock of bluntness by urging the women not to be offended by what I was about to say and to realize I was simply quoting an expert. However, some women were definitely offended, and I was uninvited. I saved the rejection letter to preserve the memory of the pain I'd felt when I'd received it. I hate to waste pain. I write my best poetry and prose during the heat of the passion it evokes.

My back began to ache as my increasing stress expressed itself in my lower back. A friend once observed: the devil loves to kick you when you're down. My world was falling apart around me.

APOSTASY

I got a facelift, quit going to church, started square dancing, bought a motor home and spent weekends camping in the mountains.

I felt allergic to church and never went again for 12 years,

Here's my line of reasoning during my "dirty dozen" years of apostasy:

1. If I'd been born again, I couldn't get unborn.
2. I'd been "Super Christian" for 20 years. I'd done more during those 20 years than most Christians do in a lifetime.

3. I'd given it my best effort and felt let down, disappointed, and discouraged by what had developed.
4. I dreaded church. I detested church politics.
5. I was tired of trying to be a good Christian.
6. I wanted to be bad and do what I felt like doing.
7. If I was going to be bad, I wanted to be very bad.

I can't do things halfway. Mother used to complain about the way I went "all out" for things and people.

My Mid-Life Crisis was launched.

I began seeing Counselor Mary. She thought it might be helpful to bring closure to the unfinished infatuation for the doctor that I'd abandoned 20 years. earlier. (A very bad idea, according to Counselor Bernadette in 2010).

I didn't know if my former lover was dead or alive. I had made a complete break with him when I became born again. I'd begged God to remove the infatuation I felt for him. But the infatuation refused to relinquish its hold on me. I felt empty and lonely for him. I called.

He was very much alive. In fact, he would be passing through Denver's airport on his way to an out-of-state appointment. We agreed to meet at the airport during his layover there. I wasn't even sure I'd recognize him after 20 years.

It all began again and continued for 12 more years until the moment I sat crying on my packing boxes in Michigan and heard God saying, "Bonnie, would you like to start over again with Me?"

HOSPITALITY

As I look back at my twelve years of running away from God and trying to live as though He did not exist, I am amazed and humbled at His faithfulness and refusal to leave me. He held me tight in His grasp despite my rebellion. He kept sending people to find a landing place in our home. Our gift of hospitality continued supernaturally. The Bible says that the gifts of God are without repentance. He gives "for keeps." We constantly had people living with us or staying for a few nights in our extra bedroom. We kept a guest book during our eighteen years in

Colorado, and when I read the entries, I couldn't even remember many of the house guests the Lord had sent into our home.

During the 1960's within the first year or two of our new life in Christ we had had people temporarily living with us in our extra bedroom. It was consistently a pleasure and not an imposition. It bothered our parents because they felt that we were being taken advantage of, but Dick and I were united in our commitment to extreme hospitality. We joked about "Hains' Happy Little Hotel" where the price fit every budget.

One benefit we experienced was that we tended to be on our best behavior when there were other people around. So our impatience and other natural inclinations were curbed and disarmed by the presence of our guests.

However, our God is a jealous God, and He refuses to let us be content when He is relegated to lesser position in our devotions. I cried a lot during those twelve years of apostasy. I never knew when unbidden, distressing tears would flow again.

Chapter 9

BEGINNING AGAIN

*W*hen I heard God ask me if I wanted to start over with Him again, it seemed too good to be true that God wanted me back! It wasn't too late to start over again with Him!

Dick had retired, and we had moved back to Mears, Michigan.

I felt at a loss concerning what books were now being written by which Christian writers. I wondered what songs were being sung. Delores, a friend of mine in Colorado sent me a Celebration Hymnal. It seemed strange to see Gaither songs in it. Gaithers had been favorites of mine and relatively new when I had left church.

The same Colorado friend sent me new books by authors who were new to me. She sensed what I was ready to read and sent it to me. I sent her checks, and she sent me more books. Her unique book ministry to me has continued since it began in 1997. When her books arrive in the mail, Dick and I mutually devour them and benefit from them.

I don't have to go to a city to find a bookstore or online to see what's available. And when I want additional copies to give away (which seems to be another unique ministry the Lord has assigned to me), my dear Delores in Colorado gladly arranges to have them sent right to our rural mailbox in the boondocks of Michigan.

We began attending Mears Community Church a half block away from our new home in my old hometown, Mears.

It felt absolutely wonderful. It was like coming home after a long journey to a foreign country.

It was the same Mears Methodist Church, but was now known as the Mears Community Church where I'd first heard that Jesus loved me and was coming to get me and I should be watching and waiting for His arrival.

It was the church where my Sunday School teachers had loved me and kept me wanting to be there every single Sunday morning for 15 years.

It was the church where Dick and I had been married in our picture-perfect wedding 42 years earlier.

Our lives were back on track and we were back in church every time the doors were open.

Most of the people currently attending my old Methodist Community Church were Reformed and Christian Reformed retired couples who spent summers in their Michigan lake homes near Mears. Most of them went south during the winter.

The present pastor came from a Reformed background. One Sunday he announced a meeting for people interested in having the church become non-denominational.

Because we had had such a positive experience when our Milwaukee Baptist Church had become inter-denominational, we felt drawn to become part of the inter-denominational movement.

After all, Jesus wasn't a Catholic or Calvinist or Lutheran, and as Pastor Bob loved to joke: "it wasn't John the Methodist."(it was John the Baptist)."

We went out of town for Christmas that year, and when we returned after the holiday, we learned that a group of the non-denominational folks had left the Mears "Methodist" Community Church and were meeting in the town hall.

Church politics had accelerated during our absence, and in 1998 we unwittingly became charter members of the new interdenominational church in the town hall.

We had been very happy and contented in the Mears Community Church during the six months we'd worshiped there. We knelt and prayed with some of our old friends there and promised that if we discovered we had misunderstood God's leading, we would return.

Emotions ran high. Unkind things were said and done between the leaders of the widening church split.

We hardly knew the names of the people we felt led to join in the new church plant.

The temporary preacher for the new interdenominational church turned out to be another "Pastor Bob."

This Pastor Bob intended to become a counselor and to be a pastor no more. He needed money to pay for the classes that would qualify him to be certified as a professional counselor.

He needed people to practice counseling on, and soon discovered that I needed counseling.

So I got free counseling. The new church got a very good preacher. And Pastor Bob got certified to counsel and gave up preaching in 2004.

BACKYARD MINISTRY

In the meantime things had been happening at our house in Mears. God had again spoken clearly to me that summer of 1997. He had said, "Bonnie, I want you to pray for everyone who comes through your back gate into your yard to use your swimming pool."

I could never have imagined what amazing things God had in mind for our back yard and our beautiful in-ground, kidney-shaped swimming pool. It was (as Scripture describes such things) exceeding abundantly more than we could ask our think. Here's how it happened:

We invited a girl from church to use our pool sometime. She asked if she could bring a friend. Her friend asked if he could bring a friend. His friend asked if he could bring his brother. They asked if they could bring their cousins. Before we knew what was happening, our back yard swarmed with happy children enjoying our pool. Their parents came to watch them swim and dive and have fun in our back yard in the center of the village where I had grown up.

We constructed a fire pit for backyard bonfires for informal gatherings.

Eventually we invited Child Evangelism people to come and present the Gospel and to invite the children to invite Jesus into their hearts and lives. Most of the children were unchurched and from unchurched families.

Pool Kids

The children loved the attention and teaching. They learned songs and sang them in our church programs. Their parents came to church to see their children perform.

Church friends invited the children to their lake homes for outings. A retired teacher came to our house to tutor children with learning difficulties. Church folks brought treats and snacks to our back yard for the children.

Our daughter-in-law brought her hairdressing skills and tools from Chicago to our back yard and gave free haircuts to all comers. Our sons who had graduated from Colorado Institute of Art made caricature portraits of the pool kids and their parents. Pool kids competed to be the first ones into the pool in April and the last ones in before we closed the pool for the winter.

A little church group in nearby Shelby purchased the old quonset hut roller skating rink to use as an outreach ministry as well as a church sanctuary. Somehow we connected with them and began taking pool kids there to skate. I got my first pair of shoe skates and felt like a kid again as I joined the Shelby skaters.

We took pictures of significant happenings and displayed them in church. People in our church chose children to give gifts to at annual Christmas parties. A special Christmas tree in the church narthex was decorated with pictures of individual children with brief descriptions of each child and particular requests for gifts and prayers.

Our doorbell rang frequently during the non-summer months, and the children visited us indoors. Sometimes they stayed for meals or sleep overs. For eight years our home was the Lord's landing place for the children of our rural community. We were "Dick and Bonnie." One little boy thought that was my name: "Dickanbonnie." When I see him in Hart now, all grown up and taller than I am, I enjoy asking him, "Michael, what's my name?" And he gets a slight smile on his face and replies, "Dickanbonnie." I love it!

Many times I sat in the back yard and prayed with adults who were there because of the pool kids. Impromptu share and prayer times increased as we became increasingly involved in the private, often tragic, lives of these people to whom the Lord had sent us.

GOLDEN ANNIVERSARY

Our Golden Anniversary celebration featured live music and a dance floor in the back yard by our pool. A friend did a pig roast and women from church served a feast to be remembered.

We patterned the earlier church part of the celebration after the Golden Anniversary celebration of old friends from the 1960's in Wisconsin. Here's what those friends wrote in honor of our Golden Anniversary:

August 28, 2004

Dear Bonnie and Dick,

At first we were going to be there at your celebration. Then I was going to do a great letter. Now it's deadline time, and we can't wait, so I'm asking the Lord for a "few good words"!

My first sight of you was summer of 1965, I think. You still had bandages on your wrist. My impression was one of big, quiet, soulful blue eyes, and your blonde good looks. Not long after, you were shooting sparks spiritually, and poetry poured out of you, all praise and wonder at God's love and mercy.

You were rushed into intense speaking and giving your dramatic testimony—very much front and center. There was no end to the Spirit-filled words that poured out of you.

Dick wisely commented to Hube and me (privately): "Bonnie's gifts don't necessarily equate with spiritual maturity. That takes time."

Those were glory days for us who were being saved then—such a dramatic ingathering of darkness-to-light ones. You were a marvel of teaching, truth, mercy, giftedness, joy, love—and benefaction to those special people God kept sending you both. There seemed to be no end to the glorious flow, to, in, and through you. And you were born to teach.

Then you were gone from here. Through the years I could see a diminuendo. You always had a talent for running your home—managing better than most. Once Nancy C., Ruth, and I stayed with you and Dick for ten days in Colorado. You seemed to handle it so smoothly. I noticed how orderly and regular your life was. You did everything well. (incidentally, thank you, beloved!)

But those depressions would intrude. You were the supreme self-revealing communicator, always bonding and identifying closely with hurting women. You didn't hide.

Dick never wavered in his role of "anchor-man." He knew he loved you and always would. He was there for the long haul "through it all" (just like Jesus). It looks like betting on you has paid off in deeper love and understanding, and the last for which the first was made—all coming out for the furtherance of the Gospel and the glory of God. He has mightily lifted you up, and your lives are magnifying your Savior together. We love you and bless you.

HAPPY 50TH, Hube and Dottie Hoff

Here's something our second Pastor Bob wrote:
Dear Dick and Bonnie,
(On the Occasion of Your 50th Wedding Anniversary)
....So it is you have moved for this fifty years. By God's grace you have done it. In spite of your humanity God's grace has done it for you. Credit where credit is due.

What a pair, the two of you! Strong solid Dick, heart breaking for the broken hearted, Bonnie writing poetry, tap dancing and relentlessly searching out the secrets of God; Dick quietly taking it all in, Bonnie incessantly pouring it all out; each a volatile blessing to each other and both a blessing to me, to the church and to the children to whom you have flung open wide the doors of your home.

Many are the times I have depended on you, and been thankful for you. Many the times I have hoped to be a source of grace from the pulpit, the counselor's chair, and the exchanges we have had in passing, in prayer meetings, in moments of shared grief and happiness, because you have been grace to me.

You shall always be special to me. And if Isaiah is right (and I've no reason to doubt he is) then someday, according to the grace of God and the love of Christ, we will look each other up on a New Earth. And I shall drink a toast of rich red wine to the both of you for your gifts to me. And at long last we shall find ourselves in a place where the world does not shift anxiously beneath our feet, and truest love runs in steady roaring rivers.,

Then, of all places and times, we shall be home. Amen, amen and amen. Under the Mercy, Bob Hitchcock, pastor and friend

Then God moved us on to the next thing He had in store for us...

MOVING ON

God told us to sell our little house and swimming pool and move 32 miles south to Duck Lake to take care of Dick's dad who was living alone and needed someone to live with him.

I told the Lord I wanted to be sure I was hearing Him right. I opened my Bible to Deuteronomy 2 and read "Move up and begin to inherit his land." I read the entire chapter. The whole chapter seemed to jump off the page and apply to us at that particular time.

It said, "For 40 years you have lacked no good thing." It had been 40 years since Dick and I had been born again in 1965.

We sold our house in Mears and managed to get our money out of it before the economic downturn that followed soon afterward.

We added on to Pa Hain's Duck Lake house, and in March, 2005 we moved in with him. We continued to attend church in Mears. Mother still lived in Mears. We were primary caregivers for her and Pa Hain until in 2008 both parents passed away. Pa Hain was almost 100 and Mother was 95.

Each Sunday we drove 35 miles each way from Duck Lake to our church west of Mears. We did it again during the week for men's and women's Bible studies. And we did it again when meetings had to be attended. We did it for ten years until November, 2013 when God opened the door for us to be part of a church 3.8 miles from our home at Duck Lake

Chapter 10

THINGS I'VE LEARNED

I carried with me valuable teachings received from our two Pastor Bobs. Our first Pastor Bob had emphasized the importance of the principle of the Indwelling Christ, also known as the exchanged life.

The Bible teaches that after we are born again, Christ lives within each of us so that (according to Scripture) it is no longer I (the old original Bonnie) who lives inside my body, but Christ lives in and through my personality, through the things I do and say as He inspires and enables me to be the Bonnie I was born to be. I am the right raw material that God is making His Bonnie out of!

We also learned from our first Pastor Bob that "thank you" is the language of faith. How do we live by faith? We say "thank you." No matter what God has allowed into our life, we accept it and say "thank you." The Bible says to give thanks in all things because this is the will of God in Christ Jesus for each one of us. It says that God works all things together to accomplish His good purposes for those who love Him.

Amy Carmichael said, "In acceptance lieth peace." We simply MUST accept what we cannot change.

Every Christmas we receive at least one Christmas card with the famous lines: "God grant me grace to ACCEPT the things I cannot change, courage to change the things I can, and wisdom to know the difference." I figure that if I cannot change something and MUST accept it, I might as well milk it for all it's worth and exercise the faith to say "thank you."

I recently learned that there are three things I cannot change: the past, the truth, other people.

When my husband prays, he always says lots of "thank you's." He and I learned from our first Pastor Bob to do that.

Our second Pastor Bob taught me to regard the Bible word "righteousness" as "right relationships" with God and other people. The Bible says to love the Lord our God with all our hearts and souls and minds and also to love other people as we love ourselves. Jesus said that those two commands summarize the Ten Commandments (NOT the "Ten SUGGESTIONS!")

I heard a speaker say that our greatest joys and our greatest sorrows come from our relationships. I know it's true. Right interpersonal relationships are key to genuine joy in living.

God has richly blessed me with wonderful women who have greatly enriched my life and development.

My Sunday School teachers Hilma, Flora and Alice loved me to the Lord during my formative early childhood years.

Alice's sister Helen became my surrogate spiritual mom in Michigan. Whenever I returned to Michigan for a visit, Helen and I loved to take a beach towel to sit on at the beach by the Lake Michigan lighthouse where we sang hymns together...including "Brightly beams our Father's mercy from His lighthouse ever more."

She wrote me long letters that I keep in a file folder and have enjoyed rereading from time to time.

Glorious Gloria graciously opened her heart and home to me and introduced me to exciting new dimensions of spiritual growth and development.

Marge C. taught the women's Bible studies that introduced me to the adventure of Scripture-come-alive.

Win mentored me in Wisconsin.

Lu mothered me in Colorado.

God has provided supportive Christ-following neighbors Rosemary and Jane right next door and right across the road here at Duck Lake.

Delores models long-distance Christian friendship across the miles between Colorado and Michigan. She prayed for me and befriended me during and despite my 12 years of rebellion and apostasy. When I came back to the Lord in 1997 in Michigan, she sent me helpful books and e-mails. Her unique book ministry to me has continued for 17 years.

Joann has been my faithful phone prayer partner since 2005.

Mary Kay, my skilled massage therapist, listens therapeutically while administering therapeutic massage for an hour and a half twice a month. What a blessing of healing and friendship she provides!

Linda, my skilled and talented hairdresser, ex-neighbor, and dear friend, lends an empathetic ear as she exercises her considerable expertise in the little salon owned by her beautiful daughter Melissa, one of our favorite, most-loved pool kids.

Counselor Bernadette is just a phone call away when we need her input and listening skills. April 28, 2014 I felt the Lord asking me to flush my ambien and vicodin pills down the toilet. Dick would have to help me through withdrawal, which he was pleased to do. Bernadette commented that this would be a "piece of cake" for Dick, after what he had already been through with me. Church friends at our new church laid hands on me and prayed for me. God has provided a wonderful support system for me.

Primary Care Physician Dr. S. takes excellent care of Dick and me. She says we are her favorite patients!

Daughter-in-law Maria is my faithful ally and confidante in family affairs and concerns.

Dick's sister Marylyn models the kind of woman I want to become.

As the years have flown by I've grown close to my dear "little" sister whom I named Connie (to rhyme with Bonnie) when I was almost twelve.

Thank you, God, for these blessed women who continue to bless me in my old age.

GOD'S BEST GIFT OF ALL

Except for the Lord Jesus Christ, my husband has been God's very best gift for me. Dick has remained steadfastly faithful despite my infidelities. He has been the anchor that kept me from flying away into the craziness that threatened everything he held most dear.

I've known him for 62 years and have never seen him lose his temper or be deliberately unkind.

2013

His quiet faith continues to cushion the roller-coaster ride I've imposed upon his steady, sensible pace of daily life. He is safe and reliable in a dangerous, unreliable world.

Our sons adore and admire their father.

I am increasingly thankful for him and our marriage. From eighteen to eighty he has been my lover and champion.

Since I am a writer and a talker, and my husband has become increasingly hard-of-hearing, we have discovered an effective way to improve our communication: once a day, usually in the morning after breakfast, he puts in his hearing aids and sits down with me and reads out loud to me something I have recently written during my personal quiet times. This puts us on the same page, simultaneously attending to the same subject.

I feel "listened to," heard, and appreciated (which is very important to me), and he enters into my stream of consciousness which is so very different from his.

I make a conscious effort to obey Philippians 4:8 and fix my thoughts upon good things, positive things, uplifting things, and things that are praiseworthy. It's like setting my inner GPS to be focused for the day. I know that whatever has my mind has me. Where my thoughts go, my feelings follow. When Dick goes there with me, we become increasingly intimate and "one."

After he reads aloud from my most recent written ramblings of my personal quiet times, he reads aloud from Beth Moore's "Praying God's Word" daily devotional book. Then he reads aloud from an inspirational book we are both interested in. Lately we've been enjoying and learning from Andrew Farley's books.

Finally, we join hands and pray for each other and our sons and grandchildren and daughters-in-law. We pray for our extended families and other mutual concerns. We commit the day to the Lord and thank Him for all He will include in it. Then Dick takes out his hearing aids that uncomfortably plug up his ears. And I go about my day as he goes about his.

SO THIS IS LOVE!

I've come to understand that the opposite of love is not hate. The opposite of love is to ignore. Expressing love necessarily involves paying attention. Paying attention communicates love. I feel loved by my husband after our morning sessions of his undivided attention.

When I feel loved, I feel open, responsive, and free to be my best possible self. Dick gets a happy wife, and it all works together to testify to the Lord's enabling us to experience an increasingly happy marriage that encourages other marriages.

Our niece Mardi is a published author and recipient of numerous awards for her writing skills. She generously reviewed my manuscript and offered comments and suggestions. At this point in my story she posted a question: "What about what you give back to him?"

I sometimes tease him (and he doesn't deny it) that what he really wants from me is Betty Crocker and Marilyn Monroe. He loves my cooking, baking, and housekeeping skills. And he loves my sexiness. He tells me he's proud to have a beautiful wife.

Another one of our inside jokes is that I am his "idea" person. I have the ideas or dreams, and he makes them come true. He's an expert woodworker, and his workshop has been the scene of his making many of my ideas become practical realities.

Together, we make a real good team. We're increasingly aware of how thankful we are to have each other to grow old with.

It's true that the couple who prays together stays together. We've just had our 60th anniversary, and we are truly more in love in our 80's than we were during our exciting 1950's beginnings.

To God be the glory (He gets all the credit).

We have barely begun to scratch the surface of the depth of the riches of Christ Jesus, our Savior and Lord.

HYMNS IN THE NIGHT

Three years ago I woke up during the night while it was still dark outside. I got up and went to my prayer chair in the piano room. The room began to glow with an unfamiliar light. I didn't want to turn on a light because I was afraid the unusual glow would disappear.

I looked up at the ceiling, and it seemed to be papered with glowing wallpaper that matched the walls and the floor.

I slowly shuffled, feeling my way in the darkness until I was in my bathroom next to our bedroom.

The walls, floors, and ceilings in both rooms were glowing with the same "wall paper" I'd discovered in the adjoining piano room. Even the windows and doors were covered the same way.

I squinted my eyes and leaned close enough to see the pattern on the "wall paper." It appeared to be old-fashioned black and white sheet music with beautiful calligraphy and decorative scrollwork design.

I leaned as close as I could and discovered the sheet music contained the words and piano notes of the old hymns I'd been singing during my several decades of spiritual journeying.

The Lord seemed to be saying to me that He was going to show me the doors and windows to the world outside my black and white hymn-enclosed rooms.

I woke up Dick to see what I was seeing. He could not see it. When I turned on the lights, the unusual glow disappeared, and everything returned to normal.

NEW SONGS, NEW CHURCH

Two years or so ago when our neighbor Jane's husband died suddenly and unexpectedly, she began visiting various churches near our homes on Duck Lake Road. She discovered a church that really appealed to her and enthusiastically told us, "I like the way they do church!"

Last November she invited us to visit that church with her, and we too "liked the way they did church."

Even the praise songs appealed to me as they had never appealed to me before. The praise band and song leaders made the rafters ring with joyful praise to our God. Old hymns comprise half the music. We feel at home there.

The church had been without a pastor for over a year. An interim pastor arrived two weeks after our first visit. The Lord has used Pastor Ron to stretch my spiritual boundaries and locate some of the doors and windows in my black and white hymn-encased spiritual rooms.

As the old hymn "Great is Thy Faithfulness" expresses so well, "All I have needed, Thy hand hath provided. Strength for today and bright hope for tomorrow. Blessings all mine with ten thousand beside." Pastor Ron has been God's man in the pulpit for Dick and me at this juncture of our spiritual journey.

An old praise song celebrates this phenomenon of God's workings in people's lives: "God hath brought us from a mighty long way..."

And we know that we have only just begun! Eternity beckons, and we follow the Spirit's directive: "This is the way. Walk ye in it."

SELECTED POEMS BY BONNIE

THANK YOU GOD

I like the life You've planned for me!
Thank you, God.
I like to live abundantly!
Thank you, God.
Your grace, Your love that made me free,
Your faithfulness, Your constancy,
The very life of Christ in me!
Thank you, God.
I like Your keeping day by day.
Thank you, God.
I like the peace that's come to stay!
Thank you, God.
The way You answer when I pray,
My sins forgiven without delay,
Christ's life in me that's come to stay!
Thank you, God.
I like believing what is true.
Thank you, God.
I like commitment full to You.
Thank you, God.
My life now bright, no longer blue,
My thoughts, my words, and all I do
Controlled by Christ within and through!
Thank you, God.
I like the life You live through me!
Thank you, God!
I like to live expectantly!
Thank you, God!
The way You do what could not be;
Your seeking, saving love through me,
Rejoicing, thanking, must I be!
Thank you, God.

COVENANT-KEEPING GOD

God commits Himself without reserve…it's not about what we deserve.
He sets a course and follows through. There's nothing left for us to do.
God reaches out to draw us in. He knows how lost we are in sin.
He sees us turn away and hide from Him who chose us for His bride.
He calls to us in tender tones. He calls by name; each name is known.
He touches us in our distress. He never ever loves us less.
He knows we're deaf and blind and lost.
He paid the price salvation cost.
He opens up our eyes to see the plans He has to set us free.
He opens up our ears to hear. He sees us turn away in fear.
He gives us gifts to win our hearts.
He grieves when we ignore, depart.
Though we struggle and resist, His love and mercy still persist.
He wipes away our sin and shame. He gives us each His family name.
He comes to us in death's cold sleep.
He comes His covenants to keep.
He knows we're born with spirit-death.
He breathes in us His Spirit-breath.
He loves to open up our eyes. He loves to help us realize
The wonders He's prepared for us, the ways in which He cares for us.
When He commits, He follows through.
There's nothing left for us to do
But learn to trust and to obey and let Him lead us in His way.
It's not about what we can earn. It's all about the love we spurn
Until He wakes us from our sleep to know the covenants He keeps.
He comes to earth from Heaven's throne.
He comes to make His bride His own.
He sweeps her off her earthy feet into the clouds the Lord to meet.
It's strange, we struggle and resist.
It's sad how much we all have missed.
It's joyful though, for me and you that what He says is what He'll do.

BIBLE READING

If someone would have told me a few short weeks ago
That reading in the Bible could be a thrill to know,
I'd have said without reserve, reply would not come slow:
"You don't know what you're saying. This thing could not be so."

Well, I am here to tell you the Bible IS a thrill!
(To those who read with guidance: the Spirit of God's will.)
It doesn't take much knowledge, but you must be very still,
Allow the Holy Spirit your yielded mind to fill.

And the pages will unlock, make clear for you to see
A new dimension of God's plan He has for you and me.
Skeptical? So was I! But this miracle CAN be!
I've seen it work for others. Praise God! It works for me!

CONCERNING A POTTED PLANT

*(This poem accompanied a plant I started from a slip from my plant.
I gave both to Gloria sometime in spring, 1965:)*

A thing that grows, possessing life, must be a miracle from God.

*Though man aspires, he can't create the spark of life anew from sod.
Manipulation of such life through work and care is man's estate.
With such he must content himself, imperfect knowledge be his state.*

*The man with faith accepts his lot and spends his life to nurture life,
Thanks God for gifts of life in trust, at times yet wastes these gifts in strife.
So friendship too, it seems to me, is of itself a living thing
Requiring work and care to grow to add to life the joy it brings.*

*All living things must grow or die, regardless of the forms they're in.
This plant, our friendship, given care will grow in beauty from within.*

BIBLE STUDY

Do questions nag your yielded mind?
Are answers what you wish to find?
Are things unclear, you would find out?
Like Thomas, are you touched with doubt?
Do you know well your God and King?
Would you discover hidden things?
Do you desire God's will to do?
Would you learn of His plan for you?

How can you hope to know His will,
If earthly things your mind do fill?
The Bible holds each hidden truth.
Or do you hold yourself aloof?

His truth you must sincerely seek,
If you would hear God to you speak.
Is your attitude: "What's the use?"
Is busyness your poor excuse?

We find the time for what we hold
Of true importance, when all's told.
If you don't study, you don't give
Your God a chance through you to live.

The Holy Spirit fills our need
Of understanding what we read.
But read God's Holy Word we must.
It's ours from Him: a sacred trust.

EMPTINESS

Try to pretend it isn't there, that the emptiness doesn't exist.
And just ignore the tears that rise to cloud the eyes with a mist.
And just ignore that gnawing ache that ill becomes you so.
Just smile and choose a better way for all your thoughts to go.
And don't give way to cancerous thoughts that eat away the soul.
Struggle to redirect those thoughts, and will your heart be whole.
Never hurt the ones you love with careless words set free.
Struggle to control your tongue. Don't let your mind think always "me."
Oh God, I think my heart will break. My desires will not abate.
I'm full, so full, of selfishness. My love turns into hate.
The strength to rise escapes me. The will to live grows faint.
I need to turn from myself away to bind willfulness with restraint.
But that first step is hard to take. The ego shrinks from giving up.
The self decries surrender that would remove pride's bitter cup.
I know the way requires this step. And this step holds me back.
Standing always just between life's brightness and my black.
My will begs me to wait awhile, to not surrender self.
Self-will, as with all, hates to die, fights being placed on a shelf.

I'VE FOUND

I've found what life is about!
I've found what I was searching for!
I've found a belief that I live by!
I've found One I can safely adore!
I've found One I can trust and obey.
I've found a reason for people to be.
I've found an interest I never can lose.
I've found in Christ a Way to be free.
I've found a treasure of wisdom
I've found a mirror of my soul.
I've found a love letter straight from God
In His word as I yield Him control.

When it comes to planning a day,
When it comes to preparing a way,
When it comes to one to obey,
You can't improve on the Lord!
When it comes to experiencing peace,
When it comes to joys that increase,
And for faithfulness that never can cease,
You can never improve on the Lord!
When it comes to a meaning for life,
When it comes to a time of great strife,
Or to things between husband and wife,
There's no improving on the Lord!
When it comes to things great or things small,
In the spring, summer, winter or fall,
There's One all-sufficient for all"
You just can't improve on the Lord!
Life in the Lord is a thrilling thing!
Life in the Lord makes me ache to sing!
Life in the Lord, how can I contain it?
Life in the Lord, how can He sustain it?
Such joy, such peace, such love I feel!
At last a reason for life that's real!
Nothing matters but Christ and what He wants to do!
His indwelling Life living in me and through!

Here's a poem I wrote about having confidence in the Lord:

HE IS

He is my confidence. He is my confidence.
My weakness shows His strength each day.
His life has cast my fears away.
His light turned darkness into day.
My soul is filled with His praise.

He is my peace in strife. He is my peace in strife.
The turmoil rages all around,
And yet my peace in Him abounds.
In Him all needs of life are found.
My soul is filled with His praise.

He is my joy in life. He is my joy in life.
Delights of life are sweeter now.
Old things are past, made new somehow.
His life my life His joy endows.
My soul is filled with His praise.

He is the song I sing. He is the song I sing.
His life in me makes all in tune.
All nature knows He's coming soon,
And whether it be night or noon,
My soul is filled with His praise.

MULTIPLIED MIRACLES

Multiplied miracles daily are mine
Delightful in detail truly divine.
He amazingly answers all that I ask.
In bliss I behold. In abundance I bask.

Rejoicing, receiving His best! And it's free!
Abundance arranged by God just for me!
Moment by moment He giveth more grace
As I set my eyes on His wonderful face.

I do not deserve it. It cannot be earned.
My best is so sinful. How painful to learn!
He honors His word, and He's faithful and true,
When I just expect all He's said He will do!

My need He has met. My cup overflows.
His wonderful peace, my heart really knows.
I'll rejoice and praise Him whatever befall.
For I know that my Father planned it all.

SPREAD IT BEFORE THE LORD

Problems arise without answers:
Too pressing to pass, be ignored.
There's ONE way to find an answer:
Simply spread it before the Lord!
Secret situations sneak in:
So private the sharing's abhorred.
Perfect, precious peace pours in
When you spread it before the Lord!
Tiny, troublesome times test too:
So petty, in telling we're bored!
NEVER TOO INSIGNIFICANT! (Job 36:5)
Take time: spread THEM before the Lord.
Nothing too big...nothing to small
For Christ to solution afford.
Nothing to fear...nothing to lose...
In trust, spread it before the Lord.

When your cup is overflowing.
When God's peace and joy you're knowing,
While your golden glow is glowing,
Let your thanks to God be showing:
Spread every joy before the Lord.
When overwhelmed with pure delight,
When sunshine floods your soul with light,
And while your mood is sparkle bright,
Give thanks to God with all your might:
And spread EACH THANK before the Lord.
Thank Him for every joy you feel.
Thank Him for making life so real.
Thank Him with all your soul's new zeal.
Be sure you take the time to kneel
And spread it all before the Lord.
As we share with Him our sadness,
We should also share our gladness:
Share the goodness with the badness
And when complaints we've never had less:
Spread HAPPINESS before the Lord.

THROWAWAY PEOPLE

(What this poem means: I was thinking of homeless street people at
first. They are the most obvious example of "throwaway people." Then
I thought of churches that turn their backs on ex-members when
they fail to measure up to the written or unwritten expectations of
that organization. I thought of divorces. It's so much easier to walk
away from a malfunctioning relationship than to stick with it and
accept, love, and encourage. I thought of paper plates and styrofoam
cups and plastic knives, forks, and spoons. We are a society with a
"throwaway" mentality. I tried to put my finger on the magic quality
that characterizes the people we are most drawn to. It seems to be
their interest in us that draws us. They make us feel good...or at least,
better. I reflected upon the unfairness of the advantage enjoyed by
children born into families that function in a healthy way. I observed
that it is ever so much easier to learn things right in the first place
than to unlearn old patterns and then learn desirable ones.)

Throwaway people, why are you so?
How did you get that way?
Throwaway people who can't measure up,
How did your value decay?
Has it something to do with the way you appear?
If appearance were changed, would you then be more dear?
Has it something to do with age, sex, or wealth,
Intelligence, virtue, wit, warmth, skill, or health?
Throwaway people: unloved, unclaimed, lost,
Unlovable, lonely, in turmoil, storm-tossed,
Whatever happened to negate your worth?
Why do you feel like the scum of the earth?
Why do you fail every chance you can find,
Saying the wrong things and being unkind?
Throwaway people, why can't you be
Loving and selfless? I think that's the key.
I think that it's true that no one will care
Unless you forget self and think of THEM there.
Think of them, help them, always give praise,

Thank them, encourage them all of your days.
Discover their needs. Forget all your own.
Become indispensable. Guard every tone.
Don't be yourself. Be someone THEY crave.
I can't tell you how to, but TRY to the grave.
Don't envy others who happen to know
Because they were raised by those who could show.
No use to pity yourself... "poor old me".
That will just turn off each person you see.
How can I help you? What can I say?
Not much. I'm sorry. I too am that way.

LET GO AND LET GOD

This is something I wrote to a friend struggling with similar spiritual and practical issues as mine.

Regardless of the fact that many, many "Christians" do more to discourage us from desiring Christianity than they do to present it attractively, (Titus 1:16, 2 Tim.3:5, James 1:26), the fact remains that our lives are terribly empty without Christ. I sincerely believe that a lot of Christians are as ineffective as they are for several reasons:

They have never had a good, walking, in-the-flesh EXAMPLE of another person who knew how to let Christ live the Christ-life through them. Without such an example, it is easy to believe that there is no such thing at all: that it's a lovely, unworkable idea from an outdated Bible.

Another reason stems from this first one: a person cannot share that which he does not have. Therefore there are very, very few ministers who are able to minister to others regarding it, because they themselves have never experienced it. Without good TEACHING, it is quite possible to slip away from the first beginnings of faith into disillusionment and discouragement with the whole idea.

Still a third reason that people fail to experience all that Christ intends for them is that so often people are reluctant to ADMIT that they do not have the answer within themselves. Through a misguided sense of pride, they labor under the popular notion that "I can do it myself." And when they look around and find such emptiness in others, they decide that "this is just the way life is," and they quit searching for the true answer.

However, the Bible tells us that God created us with a need of Himself. He also made Himself clearly evident through the things He created. Creation loudly announces that there must be a Creator, that all this didn't just "happen" or "evolve." (Romans 1:17-28, Psalm 19:1-4). It tells us that those who witness creation and ignore the Creator are altogether without excuse. Even primitive cultures have a built-in need for a god to worship. God made us that way. Also, He promises that we should seek and we will find. (Matt.7:7)

So the first practical step to take in stepping into the reality of the Christian experience is to admit to yourself that you don't have an answer for the emptiness you feel. This is quite easy for me and many like me. We know that we have tried our best, accomplished pretty good things (according to the standards of the world), and have miserably failed to experience an escape from this emptiness that gnaws at our insides. Therefore, admitting it to ourselves that our best has failed (Eph.2:8-9, Romans 3:23), and our best is but "filthy rags" in the sight of God (Isaiah 64:6), the next step is to admit it to God (James 4:10). Then we must acknowledge the fact that He is capable of all things and express our willingness to accept anything He has for us. To put this all in other words: first we recognize that we CAN'T but He CAN. (Eph.3:20). Then we, by an act of the will, surrender to Him ALL that we HAVE BEEN, ARE or WILL EVER BE. He will not force us to let Him have His way with our lives. We must ask Him to. We must say something like this (and mean it): "Lord Jesus, I give to You right now everything that I have ever been, everything that I am, and everything that I shall ever be. I want You to come into this body of mine and live within me and through me, because You have promised that if anyone will open the door, You will come in. (Rev.3:20) I thank You that You do not lie. (Heb.6:18), that You always do what You say You will do. I thank You that from this moment on You live within me. (John 15:1-5). I thank You that You have promised to live within me in the form of the Holy Spirit. (1 Cor.3:16, Col.1:27) I thank You that for You all things are possible. I thank You that You have promised to lead me into all truth. (John 16:13, 1 Cor.2:12). Now I trust You to teach me what You would have me to know from Your Word, which is truth. I thank You that Your Word is relevant to us today, (Matt.24:35), that Christ is the same yesterday, today and forever (Heb.13:8, 1Peter 1:25), no matter what some people may say or think. I go to Your Word now, and I thank You IN ADVANCE for what You have there for me today. Also, I thank You that since my life is now completely Yours, that nothing can happen to me except that which You cause or allow to happen. (1 Thess.5:18)

Then you are committed! If there is someone with whom to share this commitment, that is good. Otherwise you are apt to more easily slip away from it. I was so fortunate to have found the pastor of the the girl who lives upstairs. I called him (sight unseen) when I made my decision. He set me on the right path. The wrong, too-liberal pastor could be very discouraging to you.

The first thing then is to just be still. (Psalm 46:10), to quit all activities except those most urgent and necessary. Be very quiet, open and yielded for the Lord to reveal Himself and His will for your life. Page through your Bible, scanning until something catches your attention. Pretty soon you will find your attention absorbed in that which He has for you at that time. (James 2:22) Read, study, memorize, meditate. "Thy Word have I hid in my heart that I might not sin against Thee." (Psalm 119:11) Sin cuts off our fellowship with God.

It is important to confess sin the instant we are aware of it. (James 4:17). A friend called it "keeping a short account with God." Then along with confession comes the TURNING AWAY from that sin. God has promised to forgive and forget (1 John 1:9). And what God forgets, we have no right to remember. No more guilt-feelings! We have no right to feel guilty about forgiven sin. It would be like calling God a liar: "God, I know You promised to forgive my sins, but I just can't believe that You would do what You said You would do." How ridiculous!

Keep this thought in mind: "whatever has your mind, has you." To a large extent we can control our thoughts. I like to say memorized Bible verses to myself to "switch off" sinful thoughts. It is not possible to think about two things at once. Over and over the Bible tells us to forget our old lives, because we are new creatures in Christ.

Start every day with a prayer of thanks, starting with the fact that He lives within you and has a plan for your life. Thank Him for what He is going to do each day. Don't beg or order Him around. (James 4:7) Just ask Him to have His will done. (James 4:14, 15). Thank Him even for things that you don't particularly like, because when your life is His, all things happen for a reason...His reason, and it therefore has to be a good reason! (Romans 8:28) Consciously give Him the right to EVERY THOUGHT you'll think that day, to EVERY WORD you'll say and to EVERY BIT OF YOUR BEHAVIOR (Psalm 19:14)

When a difficult situation occurs, just pray something like this: "Lord Jesus, I don't know what this situation means, but I thank You that You do, and I commit it to You. I am completely unable to cope with this situation, but I know that nothing is beyond Your power. I therefore expose this situation to Your all-sufficiency. (1 Peter 5:7) In myself I can do nothing but fail. You can do everything. Thank You for what You are going to do with this situation." (2 Cor. 12:9) Then, once you have committed a situation to Him, keep your cotton-pickin' hands off of it! Don't keep snatching it back to dwell upon and worry about. You have given it to Him, so let Him deal with it. You've already admitted to Him that you can't do anything to improve it anyway. And He WILL! That's the most amazing thing of all! You learn to expect this after you discover His faithfulness to do all He's promised to do. I'm sure that you have a good idea of many of the "unsolvable" situations I've committed to Him, and I sincerely declare to you that He always provides that needed solution. He has promised to complete the good work He has started in each of us, so we don't need to worry about His getting tired of fooling around with us and deserting us. (Phil. 1:6, Heb. 12:2)

Since I took Him at His word when He said that "whosoever will may come," my life has been so happy, peaceful, and full of meaning. I anticipate the day when you too will experience life as it was meant to be, planned by the God who made us all and has given us the opportunity of becoming the children of God and joint-heirs with Jesus Christ. (Romans 8:14)

LET GO AND LET GOD
(How to do it)

"Let go and let God," I've heard people say.
It sounds good, as far as it goes.
But a lot of problems get in the way.
Self is one of the strongest foes.

"Let go and let God." It's great if you can.
I tried to for quite a long while.
Frustration faced me each try I began.
Failure followed most every trial.

"Let go and let God," Now I'll tell you how.
There's ONE thing you simply must do:
Say "Thank you, Lord, that You live IN me now.
Thank you that You live THROUGH me too."

Simply thank Him for these facts that are true.
Thank Him that you can't, but He can.
Thank Him for all that He's going to do.
Confess that you don't understand.

Quit all your busyness, and just be still:
Be available for His use.
Allow Him all thoughts of your mind to fill.
And thereby His control induce.

Thank Him for all He has promised to give,
As written in His Holy Word.
There's no need to BEG as long as you live.
Be still and let His will be heard.

For God cannot lie. He's the Essence of truth.
He gives all He said He would give.
Take Him at His word. He'll not stand aloof.
Abundant the life you will live!

His wisdom will guide you through every day.
Christ's patience is yours to employ!
Christ's Own love flows through these temples of clay.
Also Christ's strength, Christ's peace, Christ's joy.

ALL spiritual blessings are yours through Him.
With THANKS, you need only ACCEPT.
Christ's Vine-Life through you, the branch, will begin.
He'll exceed all that you expect!

Bonnie Hain (3-10-66)